More Praise for *The Reunited States*

"In this brilliant and practical manifesto, Mark Gerzon shows us why and how to work together for the good of the nation."
—**William Ury, coauthor of *Getting to Yes* and cofounder of the Harvard Negotiation Project**

"*The Reunited States of America* is a primer on citizenship. Read it with curiosity about how *you* make a difference."
—**Debilyn Molineaux, President, Coffee Party USA**

"This book helps us find our way back to the spirit of America."
—**Dan'l Lewin, Corporate Vice President, Microsoft**

"Mark Gerzon's clear and insightful book plugs a gaping hole in the boat of our democracy. He explains how and why we have crashed into the shoals of partisan rocks and provides a compelling case for how to right the sails and navigate our way back to greatness."
—**Mark McKinnon, cofounder of No Labels and former chief media advisor to President George W. Bush**

"Because of his passion for democracy, Mark Gerzon identifies the uncomfortable challenges that we have to confront in order to change the culture of politics."
—**Jacqueline S. Salit, President, IndependentVoting.org**

"There are lots of reasons to feel bad about national politics. Mark Gerzon provides some well-thought-out, reality-based reasons to feel better—if we're willing to take the necessary steps. This is a realistically positive and useful book."
—**James Fallows, national correspondent, *The Atlantic***

"This is why Gerzon's book is so important: it offers us visions, practices, maps, and models to help us light our path forward."
—**Michael D. Ostrolenk, cofounder of the Liberty Coalition**

"*The Reunited States of America* is a must-read—a path-finding book that will appeal to everybody regardless of political persuasion."
—**David Williams, President, Taxpayers Protection Alliance**

"As a millennial I'm fed up with the manipulation of both parties, and my generation has been hungry for something beyond complaining and protesting. I welcome *The Reunited States of America* with gusto

because it *finally* leads us toward real problem solving."
—**Erik Fogg, coauthor of** *Wedged*

"Mark Gerzon, one of the leading mediators of our time, draws on decades of experience in this book to illuminate a pathway out of what may be the country's single greatest problem today: the extreme partisanship and disrespect that has made it almost impossible for Americans to work together."
—**David Bornstein, author of** *How to Change the World*

"In our civic engagement work, we focus on building authentic relationships between people who vote and think differently than each other—a surprisingly unique proposition in today's fractured political culture. We can hold our convictions while appreciating other views. Gerzon illustrates that hyperpartisanship is not patriotism. Loving our country demands independent thinkers willing to move forward together. Mark Gerzon shows us that this does not make us vulnerable. It makes us stronger."
—**Michele Holt-Shannon, Associate Director, New Hampshire Listens, Carsey School of Public Policy, University of New Hampshire**

"Because we are paralyzed by polarization and attack politics, many of us feel we have lost our way as a country. Gerzon's book is the exciting opening chapter as we, the American people, begin to find our way back. Read it: for your children, for the rest of us—for yourself."
—**Peter C. Goldmark, Jr., former President, The Rockefeller Foundation**

"*The Reunited States of America*, for the first time in recent memory, offers our country a sorely needed third narrative. Narratives #1 and #2 say, 'Join our side and we'll fix it.' Narrative #3 says, 'It's going to take all of us working together to fix it.'"
—**John Steiner, cofounder of The Bridge Alliance and Citizen Summit 2016**

"Mark Gerzon offers us the clearest diagnosis yet of the disease of hyperpartisanship that afflicts American democracy as well as the necessary cure. He brilliantly illuminates our path forward into healed relationships and healthy democracy by focusing on inspiring tales of breakthrough success and how they happened. It's a heartwarming antidote to cynicism, polarization, and apathy, as well as a clarion call for us to embrace our entire American family."
—**Stephen Dinan, CEO, The Shift Network, and author of** *Sacred America*

THE
REUNITED
STATES OF
AMERICA

THE
REUNITED
STATES OF
AMERICA

HOW WE CAN BRIDGE
THE PARTISAN DIVIDE

MARK GERZON

Berrett–Koehler Publishers, Inc.
a BK Currents book

Berrett-Koehler Publishers, Inc.
1333 Broadway, Suite 1000, Oakland, CA 94612-1921
Tel: (510) 817-2277   Fax: (510) 817-2278   www.bkconnection.com

Ordering Information
Quantity Sales. Special discounts are available on quantity purchases by corporations, associations, and others. For details, contact the "Special Sales Department" at the Berrett-Koehler address above.

Individual Sales. Berrett-Koehler publications are available through most bookstores. They can also be ordered directly from Berrett-Koehler:
Tel: (800) 929-2929; Fax: (802) 864-7626; www.bkconnection.com

Orders for College Textbook/Course Adoption Use. Please contact Berrett-Koehler: Tel: (800) 929-2929; Fax: (802) 864-7626.

Orders by U.S. Trade Bookstores and Wholesalers. Please contact Ingram Publisher Services, Tel: (800) 509-4887; Fax: (800) 838-1149; E-mail: customer .service@ingrampublisherservices.com; or visit www.ingrampublisherservices .com/Ordering for details about electronic ordering.

Berrett-Koehler and the BK logo are registered trademarks of Berrett-Koehler Publishers, Inc.

Printed in the United States of America
Berrett-Koehler books are printed on long-lasting acid-free paper. When it is available, we choose paper that has been manufactured by environmentally responsible processes. These may include using trees grown in sustainable forests, incorporating rec ycled paper, minimizing chlorine in bleaching, or recycling the energy produced at the paper mill.

Library of Congress Cataloging-in-Publication Data
Name: Gerzon, Mark, author.
Title: The Reunited States of America : how we can bridge the partisan divide / Mark Gerzon.
Description: First edition. | Oakland, CA : Berrett-Koehler Publishers, Inc., 2016. | Includes bibliographical references.
Identifiers: LCCN 2015036711 | ISBN 9781626566583 (pbk. : alk. paper)
Subjects: LCSH: Political culture–United States. | Polarization (Social sciences) | Divided government–United States. | Citizenship–United States. | Right and Left (Political science)–United States. | United States–Politics and government–21st century.
Classification: LCC JK1726 .G47 2016 | DDC 320.50973–dc23
LC record available at http://lccn.loc.gov/2015036711

First Edition
21 20 19 18 17 16   10 9 8 7 6 5 4 3 2 1

Interior design: Laura Lind Design   *Edit:* Elissa Rabellino
Cover design: Ian Koviak/The Book Designers   *Index:* Paula C. Durbin-Westby
Production service: Linda Jupiter Productions   *Proofread:* Henrietta Bensussen

This book is dedicated to those who are working
across the partisan divide to reunite America.

All of the author's proceeds from this book will be donated
to support their message and their mission.

CONTENTS

Preface ix

Introduction 1
Are We Dividing–or Reuniting?

PART I: CITIZENS TAKING ACTION

1. Reinventing Citizenship 21
From Confirming to Learning

2. Leading beyond Borders 41
From Control to Relationship

3. Championing the Whole Truth 69
From Position Taking to Problem Solving

4. Serving the People. 95
From Endless Campaigning to Public Service

PART II: A MOVEMENT BEING BORN

5. Born out of Crisis. 125
Exploring the Movement to Reunite America

6. Mapping the Future 137
Transforming Conflict into Opportunity

Conclusion 157
How We Can Bridge the Partisan Divide

Notes 171

Acknowledgments. 185

Index 188

About the Author. 196

PREFACE

WALKING BRISKLY THROUGH the room filled with almost one hundred people at small tables, I heard fragments of conversations as each of them explained why he or she had decided to attend our event. But when a young woman said that she was a national security analyst, I stopped. Since our event was about the growing partisan divide in America, I was particularly curious to learn more about why someone focused on foreign policy was here.

"My job is about studying threats from *abroad*," the young woman said. "But I'm here tonight because we Americans don't seem to be able to work together anymore. I am afraid that the biggest threat we face is from *within*."

Although I moved on, I couldn't get the national security analyst's comment out of my mind. As I listened to others share what had motivated them to attend our workshop about bridging the partisan divides, I realized that her comment summed up why I wrote this book—and why I hope you will read it.

We want to feel safe in our country. We want to have confidence in our future. We want to learn how to deal more constructively with the differences that are splitting us apart. We want our leaders to work together to solve problems and strengthen our country.

But even candidates themselves, both left and right, say the system is broken. Washington is in gridlock. Politics is paralyzed. The pages that follow don't just explain how and why we have stumbled into a political gutter of attack and demonization. They shine a spotlight on heroes who are developing the tools, ways of thinking, and organizations we will need to reunite our country and rescue the American dream.

To reunite our country, we need to look beyond the two stories that dominate political discourse:

> **Story #1:** Conservatives are right and, if elected, will strengthen America.

> **Story #2:** Liberals are right and, if elected, will strengthen America.

With deep respect for both of these perspectives, I firmly disagree. Neither of these stories reunites and strengthens America. On the contrary—both of these stories ultimately divide and weaken us.

Tragically, these two competing, paralyzing narratives (and the two parties that claim to represent them) consume almost all of the oxygen in the public square. Whatever the issue may be, the two competing armies polarize around it, even if that results in pitting neighbor against neighbor, employers against employees, family members against family members. They may be making all the noise, but they are clearly not doing their job: only three out of ten Americans actually feel represented in Washington.[1]

Fortunately, from the very roots of our culture, another narrative is emerging that appeals particularly to the other seven out of ten:

> **Story #3:** Americans can work together with people different from ourselves to find common ground that can strengthen the country that we all love.

In the following pages, you will encounter more than forty individuals and organizations that prove that Story #3 is based in fact. It is a story about reuniting America. We not only can work together—we already *are*.

We Americans are solving problems and achieving positive results not despite but *because of* our differences. Many of our fellow citizens are living evidence of this third story. They are putting country before party. They are drawing the outlines of a new political map that connects us rather than divides us. They are forming networks and organizations that are building bridges rather than walls. They are bridging the partisan divide—in living rooms and in communities, in state legislatures and on Capitol Hill.

Story #3 does not mean agreeing on everything. Nor does it mean being "nice" or being "moderate" or "splitting the difference." On the contrary, it may mean fighting for what one believes in—but respecting one's adversary for doing the same. It means knowing the difference between an issue on which you are willing to listen and learn, and one where you believe you are not. Above all, it means disagreeing strongly without ever forgetting that "they" probably love America just as much as "we" do.

The truth is, 70 to 90 of us say that we are "very patriotic."[2] That means almost all of us claim to love our country deeply. If we love our family, we want it to stay connected. Similarly, if we love America, we naturally want our country to be able to work through its deep and genuine differences and remain united.

This book is part of a campaign—not a Republican or Democratic campaign, but an American campaign; not a campaign for office, but a campaign for our country. It is about the people, some of whom are our neighbors, who are drawing a new political map that connects rather than divides us. It is

about our fellow citizens who are already reuniting America—
in living rooms and in communities, in state legislatures and
on Capitol Hill. These are, in my view, today's real American
heroes.

But let's be clear from the outset: this book is not addressed
only to the "middle" of the so-called political spectrum. It is for
citizens who consider themselves on the "left" or the "right" as
well.

Note to conservative readers
Do you want to defend values and principles that you
cherish and that you feel are being trampled upon? If
so, you will be a more effective advocate for your values
if you know how to connect with and enlist the rest of
the political spectrum. Reading this book will give you
some new tools for promoting your beliefs, particularly
with those who (you think) do not share them.

Note to liberal readers
You believe that you are on the right side of history and
that you are championing all the noblest causes. It frus-
trates you when "right-wingers," whether in Congress
or in your community, get in the way of what you call
"progress." Reading this book will provide you with
practical strategies for reaching out to conservatives in
ways that will attract more support.

Note to "I'm-not-political" readers
If you don't care about politics or are downright
turned off by it, and think your vote doesn't matter, I
respect your feelings. But the solution is not to with-
draw. The solution is to find another way to express
yourself authentically. Reading this book will put you
directly in touch with scores of citizens who, like you,
don't want to play by the old rules and who are finding
more meaningful ways of engaging.

Wherever you place yourself on—or off—the political spectrum, learning how to work *with* fellow citizens who have different views and values will give you new and better choices for how to be engaged in politics. *You will be a more effective conservative, liberal, or whatever if you know how others different from you think and feel and how to reach them.*

The great orator and patriot from Virginia, Patrick Henry, called on his fellow citizens to pledge allegiance not just to the former colony in which they lived but also to the union of states that was being born. "I am not a Virginian, but an American," he said two hundred years ago. But what does that mean today? Just as his loyalty to America transcended his loyalty to his state, how do we rise above our loyalty to our ideology or party? Does it serve my country if I just take a side? What makes us think we are patriotic if we turn against our fellow citizens who don't share our views? *How do we love our country and still honor our own beliefs?*

In the following pages, you will meet scores of Americans who are dedicating their lives, fortunes, and sacred honor to answering these questions. They have increased my ability to deal with the complex, polarized political culture in which we live. They have also inspired and renewed my faith in our country: the Reunited States of America.

May they do the same for you.

Mark Gerzon
November 2015

ARE WE DIVIDING–
OR REUNITING?

ONE DAY, a young man named Sean Long, who had just finished his junior year at Notre Dame, visited me in my office.
He had heard about an event we had hosted on a college campus that had led to students forming a "transpartisan club" that
offered an alternative to the traditional left-right alternatives.
Sean searched me out because he wanted to tell me *his* story
and ask for my support.

"I was president of the Democratic Club on campus," he
told me. "I was sitting in my dorm with a conservative friend
who was challenging some of my opinions. We asked ourselves: What would it be like to have a safe, neutral place where
students could explore their differences in an atmosphere of
curiosity?"

When Sean returned for his senior year, he decided to
turn his idea into action. He and two close Republican friends
thought of calling it a "club for moderates" but quickly realized
that the phrase did not capture what they were trying to create. They didn't want a club, and they weren't moderates. They
wanted to break out completely from that old mold.

With these two friends, Sean started bridgeND, an organization committed to going beyond debate and finding common
ground to inspire students to take action across the political

spectrum. "We have a logo and everything," he told me excitedly, whipping out his iPhone to show me a red-white-and-blue design of a bridge spanning the divides.

At their first meeting, they were amazed that thirty-five people came—triple the number they had expected. To make sure that these newcomers understood the difference between their network and the long-established Democratic and Republican clubs, they issued a statement:

> **bridgeND** is open to all voices—liberal and conservative, Democrat and Republican, and anyone in between—willing to talk about our nation's public policy in new ways.

In order to participate, students had to accept three ground rules:

1. *Going beyond debate.* Not just talking, but moving toward action.

2. *Friends first.* Building trust and connection before taking on issues.

3. *Idea catalyst.* Creating innovative policy solutions around which students from across the spectrum could rally.

All across the nation, Americans of all ages are taking similar steps. From the Young Invincibles to Run for America to the Millennial Action Project, those who came of age in the Bush-Obama era recognized that they could not afford to participate in the left-right fistfight of their parents' generation. Meanwhile, many more mature Americans, having watched the predictable donkey-elephant attack-counterattack drama too many times, have been urgently looking for a different, better way of facing our nation's challenges. But perhaps no one can attest to the life-and-death danger of hyperpartisan politics more vividly than our men and women in uniform.

"The first time I remember being angry about our partisan foreign policy was in 2007, when I was in Jalalabad," former Army Captain Jake Davis told me recently. As the officer in charge of a tactical operations center coordinating day-to-day combat operations across fourteen thousand square miles of northeastern Afghanistan, he was troubled that thousands of troops and resources were being diverted to Iraq, leaving the troops for whom he was responsible more vulnerable than ever.

"Why did we start a war on another front when the one we were fighting was still unfinished?" he asked. "The important fight, it seemed to me, was Afghanistan. But we couldn't do it right because the resources we needed were going to Iraq."

Once he completed his tour of duty, Davis came back home and took a job with a college leadership program. He felt it was an opportunity to "close the gap between what we teach about leadership and the reality of leadership. I didn't want my students leaving our program after four years and getting lost in the same partisan turmoil that caused all the trouble in the first place."

After Davis participated in a workshop featuring speakers who were crossing the partisan divide, he immediately wanted to become more directly involved. "The perspective represented exactly how I thought our students should engage in the world of politics: being open to opposing views and learning to think critically about their own positions. It made a lot of our students more hopeful about how they could engage in politics in a way that felt more authentic. And it had nothing to do with a particular political position. Rather, it had everything to do with critical thought and an open mind."

After participating in the leadership program that Davis helped design, some of his students—both left- and right-leaning—approached him. They wanted to know how they could differ with each other without becoming enemies. As classmates, friends, and in some cases roommates, they had no interest in ending up as adults attacking each other like the so-called grownups who dominated the news. Instead, they wanted to dig deeply into their differences and emerge with better policy ideas *and* stronger friendships. As at Notre Dame, the outcome was that members of Davis's leadership program started a new extracurricular activity on campus that offered opportunities for both young Democrats and young Republicans to meet beyond partisanship and find common ground.

"The experience offers me hope," recalled Davis. "One day, if my kids go into the military, they may have political leaders who will think more carefully and collaboratively when they make young men and women bear the burden of going to war."

★

We begin our journey beyond partisanship with Sean Long and Jake Davis because they are part of the solution to the partisan divide. Like the national security analyst we met previously, they are savvy enough to know that a robust, healthy *United* States of America requires charting a new course beyond kneejerk, paralyzing partisanship.

Some of the pioneering bridge builders you are about to meet are just starting out on their journey across the divide; others have been traversing the territory between left and right for decades. Some are strong conservatives; others are longtime liberals. But all have developed a commitment to move beyond all kinds of extreme partisanship to rekindle the American genius for problem solving, creative collaboration, and civic innovation.

These diverse pathways beyond partisanship lead, first of all, through our hearts. They begin with each of us learning to acknowledge the liberal and conservative who are *inside* us. Once we have done this personal work of recognizing our own inner diversity, then the path continues—through our families (who are often multipartisan) to the Internet and social media (with all the risks and rewards of anonymity), to our places of worship (where inclusion and diversity are often a challenge), to our communities, and, last but not least, to the voting booth.

Citizens who have not been aware of this movement to reunite America may feel, as I did until recently, a deep pessimism and even despair about the negative trends in American civil life. Over the years, I have heard many of the reasons why so many of us feel that bridging the divide is impossible.

- "Now that [Candidate X] is in the race," a Democratic activist in a heavily liberal area of Los Angeles told me, "forget about bridge building across the divides. Everybody here is taking sides."

- "This election year [2016] is a fundamental clash of two opposing worldviews," a leading conservative philanthropist told me. "There is no middle ground."

- "With more than two billion dollars of negative ads," scoffed a potential funder of our work, "what makes you think a few well-meaning shoestring organizations will make a difference when the media is spewing out this trash?"

- "Don't you know the districts are gerrymandered?" said one scholar derisively. "Improving civility between politicians is irrelevant. The system is broken."

- "Look—who are you kidding?" one liberal activist for campaign finance reform told me. "When one outside funder can singlehandedly bankroll a candidate, what's the point of trying to encourage people to *get along*?" (He said the last two words with a sneer.)

- "Thank God we're superpartisan right now," said one conservative colleague. "That means maybe the government won't keep spreading like a cancer."

Everyone, it seems, has his or her reason why the partisan divide cannot, or should not, be bridged. It's almost enough to make a person give up and stay home. And of course, many citizens are doing just that. Not only do many not go to the polls, many who do feel resigned to voting for whomever they dislike least.

Those who believe there are huge obstacles to bridging the partisan divide are right. Big money, crazily designed congressional districts, negative ads, and polarized news channels—these are *real problems*. The scores of bridge-building, boundary-crossing heroes who you are about to meet recognize these problems, too.

Fortunately, even as the naysayers' voices grow louder, the movement to reunite America only grows stronger. Deepening cynicism and hyperpartisanship is one of the reasons why a movement to reunite America is gaining strength *right now*. The urge to reunite the states of America comes at precisely the time when they are most divided.

REBUILDING OUR CAPACITY
TO WORK TOGETHER

After traveling on many paths through this cross-partisan terrain, I have learned that one element is essential for Story #3. In order for us to work together with people different from ourselves to search for common ground, *collaboration matters*. The greater our capacity to work together, the more we as Americans can accomplish.

Facilitating and mediating across the political spectrum for the past quarter century has sensitized me to the importance of this invisible but vital resource. Adding in other increasingly dysfunctional dynamics—gerrymandered districts, money-saturated campaigns, "closed" (two-party-dominated) primaries, etc.—America is facing a political crisis so severe that public confidence is plummeting. Opinion polls reveal that more than seven out of ten Americans

- feel America is on the "wrong track"—the highest number on record (71 percent),

- lack confidence that their children's generation will have a better life (76 percent), and

- express deep concern about how our political system is failing us (79 percent).

Finally, more than seven of ten Americans "blame our problems on the inability of our elected officials to act effectively."[1]

When the levels of public distrust of political leaders reach beyond two-thirds, veteran public opinion analysts believe that a nation reaches a "tipping point." The country's mood becomes "volatile and unstable."[2] Voters become disgusted and cynical and stop participating. Elected officials can no longer work together. And any effort to define a national purpose, much less achieve it, becomes virtually impossible.

Beyond opinion polls, I can tell you without a shred of doubt from my personal experience that our capacity to collaborate has sharply declined. During the Clinton-Bush-Obama administrations, what unites us—respect, dialogue, collaborative problem solving, citizen empowerment, innovation—was relentlessly pushed to the margins of public life. Meanwhile, what divides us—blame, personal attacks, stereotypes, dark money—grabbed center stage.

The problem is not partisanship itself, which can work well when there is a baseline of civility and trust (as there was, for example between Democratic House Speaker Tip O'Neill and Republican President Ronald Reagan). When two people from different parties disagree on one issue, it is partisanship. But when two people disagree about everything all the time, it's *hyper*partisanship. It's not a healthy disagreement. It's a toxic feud.

Having a point of view is absolutely normal; so is organizing with others who agree. This is a natural, healthy way of being partisan: committed to advancing our own (or our party's) interests while ensuring the integrity of our institutions and our country.

However, when we disagree vehemently on *everything*, then reality itself can appear inherently divided. When partisanship becomes reflexive, automatic, and undiscriminating, then it turns poisonously *hyper*partisan. Faced with this threat, to be nonpartisan, bipartisan, or postpartisan is not enough.[3] As well intentioned as these words may be, they do not address the deeper dilemma facing our democracy.

Two comments, fifty years apart, vividly illustrate this decline in the willingness to work together in our political culture. During the 1960 election between Richard M. Nixon and John F. Kennedy, the actor John Wayne was a well-known, committed conservative and outspoken opponent of Kennedy who campaigned enthusiastically for Nixon. But after Kennedy won, the Duke graciously said, "I may not have voted for him [Kennedy], but he's president and I hope he does a good job." By contrast, a half-century later, another committed conservative, Rush Limbaugh, bluntly said of President Barack Obama, "I hope he fails."[4]

The difference between the earlier era and today is not purely about ideas. It's about attitude. The Duke felt that, as an American, he could still respect a president with whom he vehemently disagreed and expect him to look out for the best interests of the country. Like his counterparts on the left, Limbaugh symbolizes a shift in the political culture, a shift from collaboration to a fundamental, poisonous hostility bordering on hatred. It exists on both the right and the left, and if unchecked, it can undermine democracy from the inside out.

In the United States, where we pride ourselves on our vibrant civil society, public opinion analysts such as Daniel Yankelovich identified as early as the 1990s a profound "erosion of people's respect for one another." This dangerous erosion is one of the greatest concerns among the American public.[5] Never before has the issue seemed so urgent. When Americans are asked which of our society's moral virtues have declined most seriously, "respect for others" tops the list. More than four out of five Americans (83 percent) believe that mutual respect between Americans is eroding. (Also seen in decline are "honesty," 78 percent; "loyalty," 75 percent; and "integrity," 74 percent.[6])

As leaders on both the left and the right agree, it's time to "take the poison out of partisanship."[7] Two Emory University political scientists call this "negative partisanship," which they define as "voting against the opposing party rather than for their own party."[8] American political life today is a portrait of partisanship on steroids. Nothing makes that clearer than the desperate tone in a barrage of recent book titles:

Does American Democracy Still Work?

American Gridlock

The Broken Branch: How Congress Is Failing America

Fight Club Politics

The Polarized Public

The Second Civil War

The Beltway Beast

Even worse, consider the cover of the September 2014 issue of sober, stodgy *Foreign Affairs*, which featured a drawing of the Capitol building, crumbling around the edges, above the headline "See America: Land of Decay & Dysfunction."

Because this negative partisanship has been unchecked for so long, it is no longer about authentic, heartfelt differences of values and interests. It is about hyped-up, kneejerk opposition to everything the other side stands for. So intense has this hyperpartisan behavior become that it has made *compromise* a dirty word, *bipartisanship* a relic of the past, and *public service* a quaint anachronism. The poison is turning us into a country that cannot keep its promises or achieve its goals. In every election cycle, our partisan leaders once again make promises about "unity" and "working together." But the historical record shows that these promises are empty. Our capacity to work together continues to plummet.

This is why, for the last quarter century, I have focused not on helping candidates to get elected but on strengthening their capacity to collaborate. When I worked in divided communities across America in the early 1990s, I witnessed firsthand the fragility and preciousness of our capacity to work together. With foundation support, I led a project called the Common Enterprise, which was designed to bring neighbors together from across the political spectrum to decide *together* what their communities needed. I found progressive groups and their conservative counterparts working on opposite sides of almost every issue. Everywhere I looked, the left-right split seemed to have the nation in its grip. Finally, after visiting many cities, and listening to one local conflict after another that turned neighbors into enemies, I decoded a pattern underneath the otherwise-diverse disputes. I described these competing "belief systems" in a book titled *A House Divided*, published in 1996, precisely the time when hostility was increasing in the US Congress.[9]

From then until now, this "house divided" has fragmented even more. Before turning outward to America, let me briefly share with you what happened over the next two decades. My experience taught me, up close and personal, that part of the problem facing America was *inside* me and you—and so was the solution.

REACHING A TURNING POINT

Concerned about the paralyzing dysfunction on the floor of the US House of Representatives, a group of members from both sides of the aisle engaged in a quiet revolt. In the autumn of 1996, they wrote their party leaders an unprecedented letter requesting a retreat for the entire institution. As a result, more than half of our 435 representatives went away for a weekend to Hershey, Pennsylvania, to strengthen their relationship and increase "civility."

Because my work dealt respectfully with the diverse opinions present in the House of Representatives, the Bipartisan Retreat Committee entrusted me (in partnership with the Aspen Institute) with the responsibility to help them design and facilitate their historic gathering—the largest pilgrimage of members of Congress in peacetime ever. The Retreat Committee consisted of five Democrats and five Republicans appointed by Speaker of the House Newt Gingrich (R-Georgia) and Minority Leader Dick Gephardt (D-Missouri). Although the House itself was divided into "red" and "blue" teams, the committee members were thoughtful, constructive problem solvers from both sides of the aisle.

I worked most closely with the two who had catalyzed the retreat in the first place: Amo Houghton, the gray-haired Republican former CEO of Corning Glass from upstate New York who wanted a united America in order to be competitive in the global market; and David Skaggs, his bowtie-wearing Democratic counterpart from Colorado, a former Marine who quoted the US Constitution as if it were a holy book. But I also connected strongly with Ray LaHood, the influential Peoria Republican who had a way of making all of us feel comfortable with each other (even when we weren't); Eva Clayton, a tough-talking Democrat from North Carolina, the first African American woman to represent her state in Congress; and Tillie Fowler, the petite conservative Republican "steel magnolia" from Jacksonville, Florida, who would straighten my collar to make me more presentable. Completing the committee were

Charles Stenholm, the tall "blue dog" Democrat farmer from Texas who called me "son" and whose humility and homespun wisdom moved me; Jo Ann Emerson, the Missouri Republican who had run for her husband's seat after his tragic death; and Tom Sawyer (D-Ohio), David Drier (R-California), and Ruben Hinojosa (D-Texas).

For me personally, the four years I worked with this across-the-spectrum team were a turning point in my political life.

- I felt respect for all of them, not just the ones with whom I agreed.

- I found value in all of their competing points of view.

- I was moved by their commitment to transform their conflicts into common ground.

- I recognized that they had greater wisdom as a whole than anyone alone.

- I was inspired by these political leaders to believe that common, even higher, ground was possible.

As the new millennium began, I realized that, after consulting with both sides of the US Congress, I could relate positively to anyone across the spectrum. The party-versus-party, left-versus-right posturing now seemed like old computer software: seriously out of date. The committee inspired me to move beyond my own *inner* partisanship by showing me that not only was Story #3 possible, it was essential. We can—and we *must*—work together to strengthen our country.

Don't get me wrong: I still had my preferences during election years. When George W. Bush ran against Al Gore and then John Kerry, and then Barack Obama took on John McCain and then Mitt Romney, I had to choose whom I was for and whom

I was against. But something fundamental had changed inside me. For the first time, I cared more about *how* they won than *who* won. Even more important than which side won the election was how the sides would work together *after* the election.

By the time Harvard Business School Press published my book *Leading Through Conflict: How Successful Leaders Transform Differences into Opportunities* in 2006, I had worked with conflicts at every level of our society and also with political conflicts in Africa and Asia. The more I learned, the more I realized that the Founding Fathers were right: *how we deal with conflict is the key to a healthy democracy.*

DECODING THE SECRET OF
E PLURIBUS UNUM

On July 4, 1776, a committee appointed by the US Congress designed a seal for the United States of America. Although this design was not officially adopted, the phrase emblazoned in it— *E pluribus unum*, "Out of many, one"—lives on. I believe that today this phrase from our Founding Fathers still holds the key to how we can bridge the partisan divide and keep our democracy strong and healthy.

Like a secret code embedded in our nation's history, the values needed to reunite America are embedded in this ancient Latin motto. The process that this phrase describes is not automatic. Between *pluribus* and *unum* is a lot of hard work. It involves opening our minds and our hearts to find common ground. In essence, it advises us to *discover the underlying unity beneath or beyond our strong and vital differences.*

The dynamic of *E pluribus unum* is the challenge of a free people, and we rightly celebrate it. The United States of America has always had partisanship, and we have always strived for unity. *Both* ingredients are needed for a democratic republic to flourish.

What I learned about conflict is that it is most constructive, and least destructive, when it is at the optimal temperature. If it is too hot, it burns and ultimately destroys. If it is too cold, it freezes and ultimately paralyzes. What we need is conflict that transforms (or "cooks") into opportunities for positive growth, change, and innovation. *Pluribus*, the friction of our differences, creates the heat. *Unum*, our shared identity and institutions, keeps us cool. Together, *E pluribus unum* creates a powerful dynamic that is at the heart of American genius.

In the context of this book, *pluribus* (Latin, "more, many") is about the *freedom* to be partisan, to think for oneself, to make up one's own mind, and to be different. It celebrates the many, honors differences, and contrasts one view with another. It is about *loyalty* to one's own beliefs and traditions, *passion* about advancing one's own cause, *firmness* in taking stands on issues, and *commitment* to support the candidate one prefers. These are fundamental rights of American citizens and an essential part of being both an active citizen and a healthy partisan.

The differences that emerge from this *pluribus* cycle are part of the rowdy, messy civic life of a free democracy. Citizens, numbering three hundred fifty million, will always differ about what is "right." We will always struggle for control. We will always take positions. And we will always campaign for what and whom we believe in—and seek victory.

This freedom to be partisan, however, is healthy when it is grounded in oneness. *Unum* (Latin, "one") is about unity. In the context of this book, *unum* means the willingness of healthy partisans to come together and work through their differences with civility and respect. It is about identifying the whole, not just one's own part. When *pluribus* (or partisan) is no longer grounded in connection to unity and wholeness, it can become hyperpartisan. Loyalty, passion, firmness, and commitment—these qualities become more extreme and lead to unhealthy, exaggerated distortions:

- *Confirming* ideological views that promote loyalty to one's values and maintain one's identity or traditional view

- *Controlling* the levers of power—state legislatures, Congress, or the White House—in order to advance our values, identity, or views

- *Position taking* that holds fast to a pro or con stance on an issue and resists any change

Pluribus
without Unum

CONFIRMING
"We are right—
and our arguments
prove it!"

ENDLESS
CAMPAIGNING
"If you want to be
on the winning
team, join us!"

CONTROLLING
"Because we're
right, we deserve to
have the power."

POSITION
TAKING
"Just listen to
me and you'll
agree."

- *Endlessly campaigning* in order to defend and promote our own or our party's positions

Clearly this extreme form of *pluribus* needs a counterweight. *Unum* is about oneness and the unity that comes from finding common ground. It is about connection rather than separation. It is about identifying the whole, not just one's own part. It consists of four contrasting elements:

- Rather than simply repeating our preexisting views, we commit to *learning* and actively seek out multiple viewpoints through a process of vigorous public deliberation.

- While respecting our own and each other's political preferences and the natural desire for our candidate to win, we nevertheless recognize that the *relationship* between political adversaries also matters because it builds the civic trust on which democracy depends.

- Instead of immediately staking out and defending a position, we focus on *problem solving*, which includes the kind of negotiation that leads not to some stale compromise but to genuine innovation.

- When the campaign is over, we ensure that the process of *governing* fully takes hold so that former adversaries can join together in effective public service.

Unum is just as important as *pluribus*—and today even more important, because it has been so long neglected.

When the two dynamics are integrated, democracy flourishes. We can bridge the partisan divide if we reintegrate these two powerful forces and keep conflict at a healthy temperature—not too cold (which leads to repression and fear), and not too hot (which leads to lawlessness and violence). With *pluri-*

Unum
without *Pluribus*

LEARNING
"I want to discover a better option than the polarized partisan choices."

RELATING
"Whether I'm in the majority or not, I know I need to work with them to get things done."

PROBLEM SOLVING
"I'm looking for a new and better way to solve this problem!"

GOVERNING
"Power is not my goal; making America a better place is."

bus and *unum* both honored, we can strengthen our sense of unity while at the same honoring the legitimate, healthy, and vital role of conflicting points of view.

When *pluribus* and *unum* are in balance, political scientists often call it *pluralism*. It is about being different and connected. It is about being many states while remaining one nation. It is about some of us disagreeing with others. If anyone "tampers with the very secret of our sauce—pluralism, that out of many we make one," warns *New York Times* columnist Tom Friedman, we are in danger.[10]

This is what is happening today. This is why we, the people, are taking action.

PART I

CITIZENS TAKING ACTION

In the middle of difficulty lies opportunity.

—Albert Einstein

MATHEMATICALLY, Democrats and Republicans are *not* the center of the political universe. A far larger majority of Americans are Independents and nonvoters. On the one hand, this can be seen as evidence of disengagement, dissatisfaction, and even withdrawal from politics. But on the other hand, this invisible, nonparty, nonvoter majority can be seen as a potential civic reservoir for counteracting the paralyzing, polarizing extremes. In other words, we are confronting a civic danger *and* a civic opportunity.

In part 1, each of the four chapters explores both the *danger* of out-of-control partisanship and the *opportunity* to bridge the divide (*E pluribus unum*). This civic alchemy occurs because of the remarkable people profiled in each chapter who are meeting the crisis and seizing the opportunity. By observing and listening to them, we can learn how to deal more effectively with the partisan tensions in the world around us—and within us.

At the most intimate level, these conflicts may be inside us or within our families. At the most public level, they may appear in televised accounts of legislative meetings, election debates, or Capitol Hill showdowns. But sooner or later, all of us are bound to encounter opinions that seriously conflict and find ourselves torn between competing factions. We will be better prepared if we know the terrain. And who better to guide us than the men and women who are, step by step, day by day, reuniting America?

ONE

REINVENTING CITIZENSHIP

*From Confirming
to Learning*

THE DANGER

Confirming what we already believe so unquestion-
ingly that we become prisoners of our own points
of view

THE OPPORTUNITY

Learning more about issues from those who differ
with us so that we can expand and enrich our point
of view.

SUMMARY

Reuniting America is about *learning*. We can't
"know" the answer just by applying our ideology.
Instead, we can learn how to harness the best ideas
and practices from across the political spectrum to
keep America on track. To reunite America, citizens
are seeking opportunities to challenge their own as-
sumptions, deepen their understanding, and expand
their perspective on the issues that concern them.
Instead of confirming what they already believe,
they are learning beyond partisanship.

SPOTLIGHT ON

Mabel McKinney-Browning, John Gable, Eric Liu,
Michael Ostrolenk, Roosevelt Institute Campus
Network, University Network for Collaborative
Governance, and the participants of the "Climate
Change and Energy Security" retreat.

THE DANGER

Convinced of Our Own Correctness

FACED WITH A HYPERPARTISAN political stalemate between the two major parties, America is desperately in need of fresh ideas and new approaches to public policy. Another generation of diehard ideologues, who simply repeat the partisan errors of their elders, is not what our country needs. More citizens getting involved just to prove themselves right and the other side wrong won't help. We will just sink deeper in political quicksand.

Yet until recently, if one visited most college campuses in America, only two alternatives existed on campus. One could join the Democratic Club, where one was tutored and guided by various liberals, including the predictable baby-boomer survivors of the culture wars. Or one could join the Republican Club, where one could be instructed and inspired by assorted conservatives, including the local businesspeople who championed private enterprise and were suspicious of government. In other words, higher education was efficiently replicating the problem of kneejerk partisanship, not incubating civic innovation. It was creating cross-generational confirmation for one's point of view.

It is only natural to want our beliefs to be confirmed. Our political, religious, and/or cultural beliefs are the cornerstone of our identity. So we are naturally inclined to want information that reinforces our existing beliefs. Whether we lean to the right or to the left, we want to think that our values, attitudes, or principles are better than our adversaries'. So we seek out information that tends to confirm what we already believe. After all, who would not rather be right than wrong?

But if taken to extremes, we can become prisoners caught inside our own closed information loop. Living in a world in which all information reinforces or amplifies our existing beliefs can freeze us in place. Although we are blessed with freedom—of speech, of the press, of assembly, and of worship—we can easily become locked forever behind the bars of our own beliefs.

In 1960, this danger was given a name: *confirmation bias.* It means seeking and valuing information that reinforces one's opinions and, conversely, avoiding or dismissing information that challenges one's views. If confirmation bias is prevalent, even a well-educated and diverse populace can become increasingly polarized over time. Confirmation bias, multiplied by media preferences and social reinforcement, has made political views in America more extreme.

The natural place for our civic beliefs to be challenged is in school. In a previous era, this was called "civic education" and was a respected part of the public school curriculum. Young citizens attended school, not just to prepare for the job market but also to learn about citizenship. But today, this kind of subject matter has trouble finding a place in the school day—and it shows. An authoritative study a few years ago revealed that students' level of proficiency was lower in civics (22 percent) and history (18 percent) than in arguably more challenging subjects like mathematics (35 percent), science (34 percent), and reading (34 percent).[1]

When it comes to the skills of citizenship, concludes a leading civic education researcher, Robert Pondiscio, American students are "alarmingly weak." As "our national store of common knowledge" about our own history and civic institutions dwindles, we are left to our own devices. As a result, concludes

Pondiscio, "we increasingly live inside our own information, entertainment, and cultural bubbles."[2]

As undereducated young people reach voting age and become adults, this ill-informed electorate becomes easy prey for partisan politicians huckstering half-truths.

Beyond education, the other arena in which our views were once challenged is the news media. When previous generations of citizens picked up a newspaper or turned on the television, they encountered information that might challenge their opinions or broaden their perspective. But hyperpartisan politics has now so effectively polarized the institutions that provide us with our information that we are far more likely to find our views confirmed than challenged. We can insulate ourselves against disagreement by simply picking news sources that share our biases.

With partisan views reinforced by an increasingly partisan media, civic consciousness can become more poisonously polarized than ever before. The right watches Fox News; the left turns to MSNBC and other like-minded sources. If one finds the *New York Times* too liberal, one turns instead to the *Wall Street Journal*. Don't like liberals? Then tune in to *The O'Reilly Factor*. Can't stomach conservatives? Then switch the channel to *Rachel Maddow*. Want serious, multisided analysis? Good luck.

Responsible journalists who used to cover stories about serious political negotiations are having increasing trouble even finding material. "We reporters used to sit outside bipartisan negotiations waiting to see the results," Dana Bash, CNN's chief congressional correspondent, said at a meeting in Washington, DC, that I recently attended. "Now we don't sit outside those meetings because they just don't happen anymore. . . . We have to fix the system because it's broken."[3]

With even our news sources now feeding our preconceived ideas, the danger of confirmation bias only increases. The less capable the citizenry is of critical thinking, the more we can be manipulated. Indeed, the art of manipulation has become so advanced that a new word has entered the civic vocabulary to describe it: *spin.*

"'Spin' is a polite word for deception," writes Kathleen Hall Jamieson, a leading expert on political communication. "*Both sides actively work to deceive the public.*"[4] Like a pitcher's curveball, the words we hear coming out of candidates' mouths are not coming at us straight. They are loaded with spin in order to change direction suddenly in midair. It's designed to fool us.

As Jamieson makes clear, it is a systematic, calculated, and highly sophisticated strategy of both parties to package communication in order to manipulate rather than inform. Citizens are consequently becoming cynical about all political communication because they fear that candidates and their surrogates are intentionally spinning everything in order to get their votes and their money. No one, ultimately, says it better or more bluntly than ordinary voters:

> "People get a little overwhelmed . . . [sorting out] what's fluff, what's been engineered, and what's actually true."
>
> —40-YEAR-OLD SALESMAN,
> GEORGETOWN, KENTUCKY

> "They'll spin everything. You've got to wade through so much muck to try to find the truth." [5]
>
> —61-YEAR-OLD WOMAN, RETIRED PRODUCT DEVELOPER,
> LAVACA, ARKANSAS

The incentives to spin in today's hyperpartisan political system—party pressure, money pressure, media pressure—are almost irresistible.

In such a political environment, how can we, the people, open ourselves to learning? How can men and women running for national office not twist facts and put spin on almost every issue? Is the pressure to confirm our own correctness in public becoming overwhelming?

"We need men and women of good will . . . building back the muscles of consensus, compromise, and solution finding," said Republican presidential candidate Jeb Bush early in the 2016 campaign.[6] A few months later, Democratic presidential candidate Bernie Sanders made a similar plea in his speech at Jerry Falwell's Liberty University. After quoting the Golden Rule, Sanders challenged "those of us who hold different views . . . [to] engage in a civil discourse."

Finding solutions? Civil discourse? They will only be achieved if we are first willing to learn.[7]

THE OPPORTUNITY

Finding the Courage to Learn

JUST AS HYPERPARTISANS extinguish the fire of learning by requiring uniformity and eliminating inquiry, civic education kindles it. The key to sound civic education is being open to views that differ from one's own.

As the brilliant report of the Campaign for the Civic Mission of the Schools makes clear, an open mind needs to be cultivated when we are young.[8] The report of the Campaign, co-chaired by Supreme Court Justice Sandra Day O'Connor and US Representative Lee Hamilton, titled *Guardian of Democracy:*

The Civic Mission of Schools, explains why our most precious energy resource in America is not the coal in West Virginia, the
natural gas in the Midwest, or the oil off the Gulf Coast or in
Alaska. It is the civic energy of the American people. If we do
not nurture and develop that energy source, the lights may stay
on in America, but there will be no one home.

"We hope to give young people a deeper understanding of their responsibility as citizens," says Mabel McKinney-
Browning, one of the key leaders of the Campaign. "Civic
education at its best gives young people a sense that they can
have an impact on their leaders and also make them more satisfied with their lives."

What has undermined its place in the school day is more
than just the pressure of time and testing; it is also fear of being
whipsawed by extremists. "Teachers are concerned that somehow teaching this material might offend someone," she says.
"They fear some kind of backlash from parents or administration and naturally want to avoid that."

In the wake of civic outrage about the deaths of African
Americans at the hands of law enforcement officers, McKinney-
Browning, the African American director of the American Bar
Association's Division of Public Education, recalls how vibrant
civic education programs a generation ago brought police officers into high school classrooms. "It gave the police officers
an opportunity to engage with students and recognize students
as individuals. It also allowed the students to understand the
decision-making process of the police officers as well as the law.
Research showed that it improved communication and helped
bridge the gap and build a more positive environment between
police and young people."[9]

The civic education that the Campaign recommends is, in
fact, a lifelong challenge. For it to remain vibrant and relevant,

not a legal cliché, it cannot stop after we leave school or college but should continue to deepen and mature through our adult lives. This requires a disciplined commitment to recognize, but not be constrained by, one's own partisan beliefs.

"Like everyone else, I have partisan instincts and get angry," admits Michael Ostrolenk, a passionate libertarian and founder of the Washington, DC-based organization the Liberty Coalition. "But a motto that I attempt to follow is: 'There are no real enemies, only future allies.'"

To open himself up to other points of view, Ostrolenk has practiced something he calls the "30-Day Media Fast." It is a practice he believes can keep our civic learning fresh. "I recommend that everyone, from time to time, take thirty days off from being right. Stop reading, watching, and listening to things that confirm your own worldviews. I suggest during these thirty days you find podcasts, magazines, or periodicals with other perspectives that may seem unfamiliar. This might not be easy, but it is an important first step."

If you normally read *Mother Jones* magazine, Ostrolenk says, then read the *American Conservative* for a month. If you listen to Fox, switch to MSNBC. If you subscribe to the libertarian periodical *Reason*, then try the *International Socialist Review*—or vice versa.

But it's not just the act of reading widely that Ostrolenk advocates; it is also an *attitude.* "I encourage you to expose yourself to new sources of information, but not with your old perspective in mind. Don't read other points of view thinking, 'Oh that's stupid, that's dumb . . .' Instead, I suggest you start to look for the partial but limited truths within their worldviews. There are some truths there with a small *t.* In all perspectives, even the ones you hate, there may be something of value. Try to find those nuggets, and see if you can integrate them into a larger worldview for yourself."[10]

In addition to trying a media fast, we can change our media diet. We can choose to watch or listen to sources of information that stretch rather than confine us. Smart media choices can help us to strengthen our civic muscles. Unlike the superpartisan media that simply reinforce our narrow points of view, the more mind-opening media do just the opposite.

In the 1980s, John Gable was a typical political operative, working doggedly in Republican politics to get his candidates elected. But then he "got excited about technology." He left politics behind (or so he thought at the time) and joined the teams that developed Microsoft Office and Mozilla at Netscape. "I realized technology could move the world and change things in bigger ways than I could have imagined. I believe technology can empower people and empower a movement to change the course of history."

Despite his usual enthusiasm, Gable's diagnosis now is that the Internet is failing us. "In the last ten to fifteen years the Internet has boomed. It overwhelmed us with noise. So we pushed back. We created a 'bias bubble' around ourselves: we do everything we can to filter out people and ideas that challenge us and only let in what we already agree with. We begin to believe that people who disagree with us are either ignorant—or evil."

Given his fervent faith in high technology, Gable dreamed of designing a new application that could counteract this kind of media-magnified hyperpolarization. "We created the political divides," he argues, "and we can bridge them. We can use media to give multiple views of today's news and issues, providing new avenues and tools for civil dialogue."

Gable wants to create an antidote for this poisonous force driving hyperpolarization, and he is addressing the core problem: the overwhelming and often one-sided information flow. His start-up company, Allsides.com, for which he now serves as

CEO, "bursts the bias bubble," presenting the news from multiple perspectives—left, right, and center—so that multiple perspectives become a natural part of our daily news flow.

If Gable is successful, his first major client will be the nation's schools. He would like all children to be able to strengthen their critical thinking by being exposed to competing perspectives on the news so that by the time they reach voting age, no one can fool them. They can distinguish truth from half-truth. They can think for themselves. And, last but not least, they can choose their leaders more wisely.

This shift from confirming to learning embodied by Mabel McKinney-Browning and John Gable is absolutely essential if we are to flourish as a twenty-first-century democracy. Recall for a moment the new narrative that is at the heart of the movement to reunite America:

> **Story #3:** Americans can work together with people different from ourselves to find common ground that can strengthen the country that we all love.

There can be no genuine, productive search for common ground without a willingness to learn on the part of *all* of us.

The Founding Fathers considered learning so important that they built public education into the very structure of our system. But learning is even more important because rapid social and technological change has catalyzed public policy choices that are new. We absolutely have to educate ourselves as citizens rather than simply repeating old left or right positions.

To illustrate why learning matters more today than ever before, let's look at two issues that are currently controversial: sex education and Internet privacy. In both cases, citizens are breaking new ground by challenging both liberal and conservative orthodoxies.

Sex Education

In the early years of our republic, when the Declaration of Independence and the US Constitution were conceived, birth control pills did not exist. Facebook had not been invented. Computer apps on which to post sexually harassing messages or sexually explicit photographs were beyond anything that Washington, Jefferson, Adams, and Hamilton could envision. They could never have even begun to imagine a world in which the following are true:

- One American teenager becomes pregnant every minute.

- Over 80 percent of those pregnancies are unplanned.

- America's teenage birthrate is five times France's and fifteen times Switzerland's.[11]

Faced with the fact that young people are having sex outside of marriage more often and earlier than ever before, the question of what our schools tell them about sex is one that we must answer. On this issue, we cannot consult the Founding Fathers. We can't take refuge in documents drafted in 1776 when it comes to whether or not birth control should be discussed in health classes or provided by school nurses. In this technological age of breakneck innovation, every one of us is going to have to think for ourselves.

Instead of learning together, partisans on both sides often resort to reciting clichéd arguments. Conservatives preach abstinence; liberals preach access to information and contraception. But this partisan ritual of being for or against sex education misses the point. Sex is happening. Sex education and miseducation (whether by commission or omission, in school or out of school) is happening. The question is: *who* will determine *what* information is being transmitted, *to* whom, *from* whom, and *when*?

Fortunately, educators are stepping forward and challenging both sides to get serious. They advocate learning together what best serves the generations coming of age in this pharmaceutical and technological strange new world. Specifically, they ask us to open our minds enough to absorb the partisan-puncturing evidence that education about *both* abstinence and birth control *together* is more effective than either alone.[12]

Internet Privacy

At the time of the American Revolution, protecting yourself from government cybersurveillance was not an issue. Horsemen with saddlebags, not e-mail or cell phones, were the primary way of spreading the news. It sometimes took months, not milliseconds, for a letter sent from some of the more distant states to reach Washington, DC. Cybersecurity and Internet privacy were not an issue in a country where the US Postal Service originally depended on riders making it through snowstorms in the dead of winter to deliver the mail.

As the debates in Congress about the USA Patriot Act prove, this issue is not a classic liberal versus conservative choice. On the contrary, at least three so-called conservative values are being pitted against each other. The first value is obeying the law, the second is protecting individual freedom, and the third is supporting national security. When a libertarian stalwart and Republican like Senator Rand Paul is on the same side as the ACLU and other liberal organizations, clearly we are in territory beyond typical partisanship. We absolutely need a new, post-ideological approach to cybersecurity.

There is no question that Edward Snowden, the young computer geek who released millions of top-secret documents and exposed the National Security Agency's surveillance, broke the law. He did so knowingly in order to blow the whistle on

"Big Brother" government snooping. As someone working for US security agencies, he knew that security sometimes requires sacrifices in freedom. (For example, as all air travelers know, intrusive body scans by the Transportation Security Agency are now required.) But if we were going to sacrifice our rights, Snowden felt, we citizens had the right to know what we were sacrificing. He was opposed to security agencies of the US government secretly deciding for us what rights we should sacrifice in order to fight terrorism.

Reading the Federalist Papers will not tell us whether Edward Snowden is a hero or a traitor. We have to weigh the evidence for ourselves. It is not a right-left issue; it is an issue that goes beyond partisanship. Whether or not the NSA should be allowed to monitor our e-mail and phone calls in order to defend us more effectively against terrorism is a decision for *our* generation.

Sex education and cybersecurity are only two of scores of issues that demonstrate clearly why learning is key to reuniting America. There is no substitute for we, the people, cultivating our own civic knowledge and resources—which is why Eric Liu founded the Seattle-based Citizen University.

"I want citizens to become more skillful in exercising our power as citizens," says Liu, who hosts a powerful event called a Civic Collaboratory, attended by hundreds of people in cities around the country. "I believe all Americans should all renew our vows to this country. That means everybody, whether on the left or right."

After his tour of duty in politics (he served as President Bill Clinton's deputy domestic policy adviser), Liu realized that leadership in Washington, DC, could never replace the bottom-up civic leadership that makes America work. "How do we bring everyone in the tent and create something together?" he

asks. "In a twenty-first-century way that activates our true potential, we all need to become sworn-again."

Yes, *sworn*-again.

Liu believes that citizenship is not just a right. It is a responsibility to engage constructively and creatively. As the Sworn-
Again America program's website put it:

> Sworn-Again America is a project to revitalize citizen-
> ship. Let's reconsider what it means to be an American.
> Reimagine what we can do to make a *unum* out of the
> *pluribus*. In ceremonies at dinner tables, block parties,
> or town squares, with five or five thousand, take the
> oath to become a Sworn-Again American![13]

From Liu's perspective, hyperpartisan politics is not fostering responsible citizenship but is, on the contrary, turning people off. Instead of thinking of politics as "bad, full of dirty tricks,
negative ads, and big campaigns," Liu built Citizen University
to "embed the idea of citizen empowerment across the entire
political spectrum." He recognizes that Congress is in what he
calls "an institutional death spiral," which is why he focuses on
exploring "the original meaning of politics, which is positive
and has to do with balancing competing interests and looking
for solutions."

Fortunately, the revitalizing-citizenship premise of Citizen
University is also gaining ground in many mainstream universities as well. Leaders of colleges and universities, as institutions of higher learning that are often supported by state
and federal funds, are becoming increasingly aware that being
bastions of conservatism or liberalism is antithetical to true
civic education. College students are eager to participate in
campus-based activities that, unlike the traditional Democratic
and Republican clubs, promote learning beyond partisan-

ship. They participate through the Roosevelt Institute Campus
Network (38 states), the University Network for Collaborative
Governance (25 campuses), and many other programs that are
catalyzing a new generation of citizens who can think beyond
left and right. Administered by the Policy Consensus Initiative,
the UNCG programs make sure that students have another
path besides the predictably polarized ones offered by partisan
political clubs. Using local issues and connecting with local
governments, UNCG institutions of higher education are acting as catalysts for precisely the new politics we need.

My own quarter century of work in this field confirms my
colleagues' emphasis on learning. Again and again, I have experienced how essential it is at every level of government, particularly at the top.

I encountered this first in my four years of close-up work
with the US House of Representatives. In one exercise, the
members themselves worked side by side to define all the
causes of rising incivility, both inside and outside the House.
When they witnessed their collective analysis, they were
stunned. In less than an hour, they had developed the most detailed, thorough, and accurate portrait of the problem that they
had ever seen. Many of them realized that learning together
was the key to reinvigorating governing.

I experienced this again in 2004 when I facilitated a retreat involving former Vice President Al Gore and his most
vehement critics on climate change. With the pain of his loss
to George W. Bush in the 2000 presidential election still fresh,
Gore spent three days at the retreat, titled "Climate Change and
Energy Security." (My colleagues and I crafted the hybrid title
very carefully to ensure that participants from across the political spectrum would feel included.)[14]

On the opening day, Gore presented his *Inconvenient Truth* slide show (later to become an Academy Award-winning movie) to the assembled group of thirty "experts" who represented opposing positions on climate change. Then a team of critics from a conservative think tank, the Competitive Enterprise Institute (CEI), who had financed attack ads attempting to discredit his work, presented their views. They explained why they questioned the validity of the idea of climate change and felt that the green approach threatened jobs, economic growth, and individual liberty. (Other participants represented a diverse spectrum on this issue, including faith-based organizations, renewable-energy advocates, and corporate energy industry lobbyists.)

My co-facilitator, William Ury, and I led the group through a sequence of conversations that finally yielded significant learning on both sides. On the final day, Gore acknowledged that he had learned from his critics how he could express his climate change views more effectively to a conservative, business audience. Meanwhile, his critics admitted that underlying their opposition to climate change was, in fact, a deeper concern: they felt the issue was being used as a "cover" for a liberal expansion of government and further regulations in the private sector.

One of the key lessons that Gore learned at the retreat was that his approach to climate change appeared to his conservative critics as just another Trojan horse for more government. Like a classic liberal, he had left his critics with the impression that government would be primarily responsible for solving the challenge of climate change. The CEI conservatives, of course, felt that if any sector would ultimately meet the challenge, it should be the private sector.

Here was Al Gore, who had spent his life from childhood on in the political realm, discovering how to communicate more effectively across the divides. It was a moving reminder that every one of us, from the highest government official to a child entering kindergarten, needs to keep learning.

I had to learn this lesson again on the final morning of the "Climate Change and Energy Security" retreat. Just when we thought the meeting was heading toward a successful conclusion, the room was torn apart unexpectedly by two men whose passionate statements exposed the deeper divide in the group that had remained beneath the surface.

"America can't be a leader in the fight against climate change," said one of the participants, the executive director of a "liberal" renewable-energy consortium. "We are one of the most hated countries on earth. We take resources from the rest of the world and then bomb countries that resist us. We are the greediest nation on earth. My kids pretend they are Canadians when they go abroad, just to protect themselves."

The anger in the room that erupted after his "anti-American" statement was palpable. To give it a voice, I called on the next speaker, the head of an association of energy companies who had close ties to the Bush administration.

"I can't sit by silently and listen to my country being run down like that," said the conservative white-haired businessman in a strong southern accent. "We are the most generous country on earth. People die every day trying to get into our country. We are beloved around the world. I am proud to be an American—and will stand up to anybody who says different."

The room erupted in chaos, voices vying for attention, hands waving wildly for recognition. The two speakers, sitting on opposite side of the room, both had tears streaking down their cheeks. I stood up and raised both arms like a cop stopping traffic and asked for a moment of complete silence. When I finally got the attention of the room, I knew that what I said next needed to be precise.

"When we resume our conversation," I said, "I ask you to remember why you came here. I ask you to hold both of these two fine men in your hearts."

After the moment of silence, I rang a bell, and a cluster of hands shot up. I called on four people to speak, making sure that the quartet reflected the diversity of the group. They each addressed in their own way the complexity of our role in the world and the terribly mixed feelings they had of pride and guilt, patriotism and self-criticism. As their collective wisdom emerged, they held the profound and beautiful paradox that is America: we have done enormous good in the world and also caused more harm than we dare to admit.[15]

As I listened to them, I realized that America could never be reduced to a positive or negative cliché. We are too great a nation to be captured by blind pride or blind criticism. The United States of America challenges us to be more than that. It challenges us to see more clearly, and feel more deeply, and continue learning how to fulfill our sacred destiny as a nation.

TWO

LEADING BEYOND BORDERS

*From Control
to Relationship*

THE DANGER

Controlling, or attempting to control, those who differ from us in order to achieve our short-term political goals.

THE OPPORTUNITY

Relating as fellow citizens to those who differ from us in order to create effective long-term relationships that lead to sustainable decisions.

SUMMARY

Reuniting America takes the idea of "loving our country" seriously—and love means relating to our fellow Americans, especially those who differ from ourselves. While of course we all prefer that candidates from our own party win, citizens today want something more. In a country more or less divided in thirds (Democrat, Independent, Republican), nothing significant will endure or flourish unless the relationships across the spectrum are strong and healthy.

SPOTLIGHT ON

Joan Blades, Laura Chasin, Richard Cizik, Sandy Heierbacher, Liz Joyner, Bryan Desloge, Allan Katz, Martha McCoy, and Doug Tanner.

THE DANGER
A Country out of Control

"Polls Indicate Democrats Will Lose Control of Senate"

"Senate Elections 2014: Republicans Seize Control of the Senate"

AS ELECTION HEADLINES REVEAL, the goal of politics is clear: *control*. It is about who will directly control the levers of our government—and indirectly control our country.

The wording of various news reports is almost identical. One party "wins" (or "seizes") control; the other party "loses" (or "forfeits") it. Partisans want their candidate, or their party, to be victorious so that the White House and Congress, the governor's mansion and the state legislature, will be under their control. The unquestioned assumption is that control is good because it will get our side what we want.

Up to a point, control is a sensible goal and a critical component of a healthy democracy. But taken to an extreme, it can become dangerous. The clamoring for control actually spins us *out of* control, usually in one of two directions. It can turn into domination on the one hand and stalemate on the other. So when government appears to be getting too much control—for example, when fears arise that security agencies are reading the e-mails and monitoring the phone calls of ordinary Americans— both conservatives like Senator Rand Paul and liberals like former Senator Mark Udall sound the alarm.

But if too much control (domination) is dangerous, so is too little (stalemate). If no one controls the steering wheel—or, more precisely, if two drivers are madly fighting for control— a vehicle will careen from left to right and potentially crash.

We, the people, want a certain level of control that ensures our safety and keeps us as a nation heading in the right direction.

The government shutdown in 2013 was dramatic evidence of stalemate. With both parties madly struggling for control, the unintended by-product of that struggle was just the opposite: paralysis. As soon as one party gained momentum, the other undercut it; as soon as one policy was enacted (for example, the Affordable Care Act, or "Obamacare"), the other side attempted to repeal it; as soon as one party's leader took a position, the other party pivoted to the opposite. Ever since then, "democracy" has functioned like a straitjacket preventing either side from accomplishing anything. The obsession for partisan control ultimately creates the opposite outcome: a country *out of* control.

This hyperpartisan way of "communicating" is now so commonplace that Americans on both the right and left do it. The result, according to Norm Ornstein, coauthor of *It's Even Worse Than You Think*, is that we are becoming "tribal." This tribalism, Ornstein believes, "has metastasized to the states and to the public." Significant percentages of both Republicans and Democrats don't want their child to marry a member of the other party. "Although it is hard to believe," asserts Ornstein, "interparty marriage is now seen as more problematic than interreligious or interracial."[1]

The quest for control, rather than a commitment to relationship, makes us communicate from a hyperpartisan stance. In the ongoing media wars between MSNBC and Fox, for example, a liberal talk show host for the former, Keith Olbermann, ridiculed a rival talk show host for the latter, Bill O'Reilly. Wearing an O'Reilly mask, Olbermann made the Nazi salute, clearly implying that his Fox counterpart resembled the fascist followers of Hitler. The incredibly insulting "joke" was so offensive that the Anti-Defamation League wrote Olbermann a personal letter asking him to stop associating his fellow American news program host with the Third Reich.[2]

Although most political commentary is not that defamatory, it is nevertheless extremely shallow and ineffective:

- *Few people actually listen.* Either the combatants shout or wait for their turn to shout. Conversation is reduced to aggressive sound bites. Facial expressions often reveal anger and contempt for others.

- *Everyone feels misunderstood.* Everyone in an argument feels stereotyped, or dehumanized, by his or her opponents. Both sides leave an encounter complaining of being misquoted, misheard, misused, or otherwise disrespected.

- *Language breaks down.* Attempts at discourse are futile because words are used as weapons, and talking makes things worse. The same charges and countercharges are repeated again and again. "There you go again" is a common refrain.

- *Person-to-person communication fails.* In an atmosphere of fear and tension, antagonists speak in generalities and slogans. Rarely do they address one another as flesh-and-blood human beings.

- *Extreme positions are emphasized and reinforced.* The loudest and most obnoxious voices capture the most attention in the media. People with moderate views who recognize the complexity of an issue and speak quietly and respectfully are ignored.

With behavior of this kind on the part of the citizenry, America is paralyzed. People are pitted against one another rather than working with each other. While the nation is not about to be plunged into a civil war, it does face a future of chronic gridlock. As a people, we are likely to be increasingly cut off from each other, separated by fear and suspicion, and unable to innovate or respond quickly. The United States could become less competitive in the world markets and less able to inspire other nations around the globe. America's famous can-do energy could give way to can't-do bitterness.

Once again, no one describes the danger more eloquently than the voters themselves. Reflecting simple common sense, in basic language that we can all understand, voters in exit polls in 2014 captured the country's mood:

> "They just don't seem to get anything done anymore. All they do is fight between each other and get nothing done. So we—and I—need something different in there. Everything needs to change."
>
> —JOHN MILLER, IOWA

> "I'm just tired of all the fighting and bickering. We're all Americans. It's getting old with all that stuff."
>
> —JEFFREY KOWALCZUK,
> RACINE, WISCONSIN[3]

Communicating to manipulate and control takes a toll on everyone. It makes citizens want to disengage from politics. And it makes candidates—and their families—think twice about public service.

"What do I tell my five-year-old?" asked the wife of a member of Congress. She was participating in the first US House of Representatives Bipartisan Congressional Retreat that I facilitated. "What do I tell Jake when he asks me if the stuff they're saying about Daddy on the TV is true?"

The circle of fifteen members of the House and their spouses sat in silence as tears streaked down this young mother's cheeks. They knew she wasn't finished. They knew there was more.

"So I told Jake they're lying about his father," she continued. "But then he asks me, 'Why? Why are they lying about Daddy?' So tell me," she said, looking desperately around the circle, "tell me how I am supposed to explain that to my son."

Until I worked closely with members of the House of Representatives, I had known only a handful of men and women who had run for high office and happened to be acquainted with a few presidential candidates. But I had never before had the privilege of hearing scores of politicians and their spouses speak privately—and vulnerably—about their own and their family's pain.

> "My kids would pick up the phone and . . . and it was just too much! We had to change our family phone number."

> "They'd write words on our campaign signs . . . words that no child should be exposed to. We'd have to take them down and try to wash them clean."

> "At first my opponent and I honored our agreement to run clean campaigns. But when the outside groups started throwing mud, our agreement fell apart."

> "I'll never forget coming out of our neighborhood supermarket. Someone had scrawled 'traitor' and 'go to hell' across the windshield of our car."

As they went around the circle, they quoted a litany of veiled insults, anonymous rumors, ugly innuendoes, and outright attacks.

Everyone at the retreat was, by definition, a winner. But like a battered boxer who barely survived the fight, they were wounded and in pain. The weapons were not fists, but words. Yet, as an election approaches, news reporters and commentators habitually describe election rhetoric with the metaphor of boxing.

In the 1996 presidential election, scandal-ridden President Bill Clinton was pitted against his Republican challenger, Kansas Senator Bob Dole. Soon after the two debated each other in Hartford, Connecticut, the press was filled with articles analyzing who won. "No knockout," said the headline in my local newspaper, a segment on *Today*, and dozens of other media accounts of the first presidential debate. They "jabbed and parried and counterattacked," summarized an article in the *Washington Post*. It was a "draw," concluded countless commentators.

In an editorial published in the *Washington Post* before the next debate, I challenged that newspaper specifically and the press more generally to become more creative:

> Come on, ladies and gentlemen. As we analyze tonight's debate, can't we find a new metaphor? Neither participant behaved as if he was in the ring. There was no bell, no boxing gloves and no blood. The final act of the event was the 73-year-old antagonist announcing his worldwide web page on the Internet. Yet the event is consistently reported as if Dole and Clinton were two champion prizefighters, as if Hartford were Las Vegas and as if presidential debates were a heavyweight title bout.[4]

What I wrote twenty years ago is, unfortunately, still true. Journalists still turn reflexively to the same cliché. Every election cycle, the same tired metaphor is brought forward by political commentators: two sides punching each other, scoring points, trying to survive their opponent's attack, damaging their opponent as much as they can, throwing punches until the final bell, etc.

Think about the boxing metaphor and tell me: Where in the ring do the 40-plus-percent Independents fit? When the entire event is about whether the boxer on the left or the boxer on the right will win, where do the rest of us belong?

A boxing match cannot manage a complex economy. This is why economic opportunity—*whether during Democratic or Republican administrations for the last forty years*—has slowly but surely been grinding to a halt for many American families. Beginning around the mid-1970s, it became harder to reach the next rung on the ladder. Economic statistics show that the rungs in that ladder got farther apart. While productivity rose during those four decades by 90 percent, the typical family's income increased by less than 8 percent. Consequently, more Americans than ever have lost faith in the ladder of success.[5]

Unfortunately, knee-jerk partisan politics and polarized media sound bites now offer only two ridiculously simplistic explanations. According to one party, the thief who stole the American dream is a wasteful big-government, entitlement-spending, job-killing liberal. According to the other, the thief is a big-business, trickle-down, 1 percent–pandering conservative. To maintain this blame-the-other-party story line, both sides deceive the voters. According to the usual script, the party in power spins the facts to make the economy look better than it is, and the party out of power distorts the facts to make the economy look worse.[6]

"The American people realize they've been robbed," concluded two veteran investigative reporters who studied the
2008 economic meltdown and the so-called recovery that followed. "They're just not sure by whom."[7]

Why did the expansion of the American economy stop
"trickling down" to the middle class and poor? Why did the
American dream for many citizens turn sour? Was it because, in
the metaphor of one columnist, the economic "escalator" broke
down?[8]

Unfortunately, we can't fix the economy, because hyperpartisan politics prevents us from planning coherently. We no
longer project authority or reliability to the other great powers. Anyone who thinks that our country is not a declining
economic power is not paying attention. Sage observers of our
country's role in the global economy witness "a United States
government so bitterly divided that it is on the verge of ceding
the global economy it built at the end of World War II."[9]

But the danger, alas, is not only to our livelihoods. In the
case of our troops, it is life itself that is endangered. As Captain
Jake Davis's remarks in the introduction underscored, many of
our men and women in uniform feel that they or their buddies
are being sacrificed on the altar of hyperpartisan politics.

Just imagine what it's like to be in uniform, deployed on the
battlefield, and hearing the kind of back-and-forth battle of one-
liners on Capitol Hill. "How did that work out for us last time?"
snapped Senate Majority Leader Harry Reid (D-Nevada), when
the Senate was debating how to confront the new threat of
ISIS in 2014. "The Bush-Cheney strategy of rushing into conflict doesn't work. It didn't work then and it won't work now."
Immediately the other side shot back: "If all [Obama] plans to
do is manage this threat and pass it off to his successor, then we
should know that now," fretted Senate Minority Leader Mitch

McConnell (R-Kentucky). Meanwhile, Senator John Cornyn (R-Texas) threw in one more jab: "President Obama's chronic passivity has helped the jihadists."[10]

This nasty, bitter, hyperpartisan sniping does not support our troops. On the contrary, it makes them wonder whether they are pawns in a political game. If we really supported them, would we be arguing like barroom brawlers about what we are asking them to do? If they are going to risk their lives, don't they deserve some clarity about why? Don't they deserve the same patriotic sacrifice from us that we expect from them?

To risk their lives, our troops want to know:

1. why we are asking them to risk their lives,

2. whether we will give them the support they need while deployed, and

3. how we will help them when they return.

On all three counts, hyperpartisan politics has undercut our promise to support our troops. As the struggle for control between the parties has turned foreign policy into another election-oriented, advantage-seeking tactic, many soldiers feel used. How can we ask them to risk their lives if our foreign policy changes every few years? How can we guarantee continued support on the battlefield if it's subject to infighting on Capitol Hill? And how can we promise them a respectful homecoming if we are continually changing our military priorities?

Not only on national defense but on scores of other issues—health care, immigration, debt reduction, educational reform—we need men and women who can lift themselves above their habitual positions and ideologies. Instead, the system now attracts partisan campaigners and repels those interested in innovative governance.

"I think the country is hungry for authentic, genuine leadership on both sides," said Howard Schultz, CEO of Starbucks, in a 2014 interview. "And until we see that, I think it's hard to be optimistic. I'm optimistic about the country; I'm optimistic about the American people."

"You're just not optimistic about the leadership?" he was asked.

"No, I'm not," Schultz said.[11]

THE OPPORTUNITY

Daring to Connect

What voters want, and what America needs, are leaders who will seek relationship with their adversaries rather than control over them. Since we are not going to have one-party rule, we need politicians who will work together. As CEO Howard Schultz said bluntly in a 2015 op-ed, "Americans who are tired of politics as usual should demand a clear answer to a simple question from every candidate: *What will you do to unite all of us?*"[12]

Those who have been close to the center of power have reached exactly the same conclusion. We need leaders who relate to each other well enough that they can solve the problems facing the country. As Tamera Luzzatto, who was chief of staff for then-Senators Hillary Clinton and Jay Rockefeller for more than a decade, put it, "Voters want to ask politicians: 'Why can't you do what I do with my husband at the dinner table? Why can't you do what businesspeople do all the time in negotiations? Why can't you work it out?'"[13]

If we want to learn how to work it out, there is no better place to start than with my colleagues who dared to connect adversaries on one of the most electrically divisive issues in America.

In 1989, Laura Chasin watched an encounter about abortion sponsored by the Better World Society on PBS. "I expected a constructive debate, but what I saw instead was shouting heads," Chasin recalls. "Viewing the tape with some of my family therapy colleagues, we started asking ourselves if some of what we did with families in polarized, stuck conflict could be used to foster more constructive conversations about polarizing public issues."

Chasin and her colleagues decided to answer their question by convening and facilitating one-evening pilot conversations about abortion with small groups of pro-life and pro-choice opponents. They videotaped twenty groups of four to eight people over the course of a year and a half. Feedback from the participants indicated that the combination of habit-disrupting ground rules, firm structure, and thoughtful questions was the key to allowing them to humanize the other side and take a genuine interest in understanding their adversaries.[14] "Those early dialogues repeatedly taught us," she recalls, "how relatively easy it can be to build an environment in which partisans shift rapidly out of their previous black-and-white movies of their opponents into Technicolor ones."[15]

After these initial pilot dialogues, Chasin and her associates formed the Public Conversations Project. Although they applied their approach to other public issues, they returned to the abortion issue after a shocking event took place just two miles away.

A few days after Christmas in 1994, John Salvi shot and killed two receptionists who worked at clinics that offered abortion services in Brookline, Massachusetts. Several other staff members were badly injured. These murders reminded the country of the latent lethality in the culture wars and created anxiety in Boston citizens across the political spectrum. Local pro-choice leaders were afraid of copycat attacks; pro-life leaders feared counterattacks.

After the clinic shootings, Public Conversations partnered with a local mediator and initiated a confidential dialogue with the major pro-choice and pro-life leaders in the Boston area. The primary goal of the six participants was to help de-escalate the polarization between pro-life and pro-choice groups in Massachusetts. They did so by building relationships based on mutual respect and understanding that respectfully addressed their major differences about values and policies. As understanding of their opponents' views deepened, the participants tempered their public rhetoric to reflect a more accurate understanding of their adversaries. While retaining their deeply held views about abortion, they also developed a hotline and took actions that may well have prevented another violent event.

One specific outcome of the pro-life/pro-choice dialogues was the realization that *relationship matters*. Once the opponents knew each other, not as stereotypes in the media but as women with children and families and jobs, they started to see a whole person. As a result of many months of dialogue, no one necessarily changed their *position*, but everyone changed their *attitude*.

What Chasin and her organization are promoting is a process, not a policy or a product. It is a process of relationship building that keeps the politics of control in balance. While the pro-choice and pro-life advocates continue their efforts to control the policy outcome, they do so in the context of a healthy relationship with their adversary. The result of a better relationship: better policies get made.

The measure of our citizenship is our connection to each other—the bonds that make us one people. Today some social scientists give the name *social capital* to the interweaving of trust, social ties, and common concerns that underlie genuine community. It is also called collaboration, engagement, revitalizing of citizenship, community building, and a myriad of other names. But, in essence, it is simply a feeling of kinship. As President Lincoln put it long ago:

> Let us neither express nor cherish any hard feelings toward any citizen who . . . has differed with us. Let us at all times remember that all American citizens are brothers of a common country, and should dwell together in the bonds of fraternal feeling.[16]

Such "fraternal feeling"—which Lincoln elsewhere called "a Union of hearts and hands"—is a kind of love. It is rooted not just in the mind or the heart, but also in the soul. It requires the deepest and most profound commitment to civic relationship of which we are capable. It requires building relationships across the divide—not in theory, but on the street.

Among organizations that are champions of relationship as a counterbalance to control, ground rules seem to be an essential building block. Virtually every project that moves beyond partisanship at the local level effectively adopts ground rules that are not about one faction controlling another but about all factions relating to each other. I have learned that this is true not only in our homes, neighborhoods, and communities, but even in the US Congress.

The key to the Bipartisan Congressional Retreats was putting aside the normal House of Representatives ground rules. Those rules are about one party maintaining control. For the retreats, we established a new set of ground rules that were about building relationship.

Bipartisan Congressional Retreat
Ground Rules

Objective: "To create a safe environment for
open conversation."

RESPECT
"To show consideration for;
avoid violation of; treat with deference."
No personal attacks.

FAIRNESS
Equal time for speakers.
Speak briefly; time is limited.

LISTENING
When others speak, listen—don't prepare your remarks.
Listen with intent to understand.

OPENNESS
To other points of view.
To outcome.
To each person regardless of seniority.

PRIVACY
Treat sessions as confidential.
Outside the retreat do not attribute comments to others.

This feature of the design resulted in part from a conversation I'd had with one skeptical member who confronted me in a committee meeting. "How can you be sure," he asked bluntly, "that we will act more civilly in Hershey, Pennsylvania, than we do on Capitol Hill?"

"We can't be sure unless—" I began to reply.

"Then why in hell are we spending almost one million dollars?" the congressman interrupted, cutting me off angrily. "Can you guarantee we won't just go make fools of ourselves somewhere else?"

"We can't be sure, sir, *unless we set some ground rules!*" I replied fiercely.

That confrontation catalyzed the adoption of a set of ground rules for the first Bipartisan Congressional Retreat, which members themselves authored and pledged to enforce. The chart shown here was posted in every small-group meeting room and (despite one minor infraction at the first retreat and two at the second) was strictly honored for the duration of the two retreats.

That the ground rules adopted at the retreat seem quite ordinary and unoriginal is, in fact, the point. As any classroom teacher or assembly-line foreman would agree, basic civility is necessary in order to accomplish the work at hand. This is even more true on Capitol Hill than in other workplaces because the pressures are so intense and the stakes so high.

Two decades later, as I look back at the remarkable quality of the retreats, I am certain that the ground rules they adopted were critical. As long as those ground rules were in force at the retreat, the members of the House acted like collaborative problem solvers working through their differences. But when the ground rules were put back on the shelf on Capitol Hill, the hyperpartisan slide into the mud resumed—and continues to this day.

To understand the power of verbal ground rules, remember that words are like weapons. "We don't just ask rival gang members to trust each other," said an African American colleague of mine who built truces between rival inner-city gangs called Crips and Bloods. "We frisk them at the door. Nobody's going to feel safe if there are weapons in the room." He was referring to firearms, not fiery language. But words can be used as weapons, too. Ground rules are the most effective way of establishing a zone of safety within which conflict can be addressed. The safer the "container," the deeper and more transformative the conversation can become.

The ground rules they adopted enabled the members of the House of Representatives to turn partisanship into partnership—if only briefly. Each of the small groups at the retreat was facilitated by one Democrat and one Republican. This cross-party pair was responsible for enforcing the ground rules. These co-leaders were full and equal partners—not a chair from the majority party and a vice chair from the minority, pitted against each other.

The simple innovation at the retreats of developing the position of co-leaders had a transformational impact. The pairs embodied the reality of collaboration. When they were incentivized to work together, not against each other, leading across the divide became an honorable pursuit. If members were encouraged to find one or more counterparts across the aisle with whom to explore strategic partnerships on specific issues, the House could be a creative catalyst for a wide range of innovative approaches to policy challenges. The goal would not be to end partisanship (that would be neither constructive nor realistic), but rather it would be to create a parallel, "cross spectrum" level of engagement in the House that would complement the usual party-based maneuvering.

Far beyond Capitol Hill, thousands of organizations at the local level are already doing this kind of relationship building work. For a quick glimpse of this field in all its rich diversity, there is no better starting point than the National Coalition for Dialogue & Deliberation.

The seed for NCDD was sown almost twenty years ago when a young graduate student, Sandy Heierbacher, decided to focus on efforts to improve race relations. To discover what methods helped—or didn't—she interviewed practitioners across the country. It was then, she recalls, that she "fell completely in love with dialogue and with the people who are drawn to this work."[17]

But as she met this invisible network of bridge builders, she discovered the weakness of the field. The practitioners were often "solopreneurs" who felt isolated and underfunded; and they were frustrated because dialogue did not often enough translate into concrete action. So she expanded her inquiry to include not only dialogue but community deliberation. She created online space for practitioners to share their experiences, and before long, NCDD was born. It is now home to more than two thousand initiatives for sewing America together, one stitch at a time.

Of the thousands of organizations, let's look briefly at three exemplary initiatives that are building relationships locally across the divides. Each has proved why relationship building produces breakthrough results.

Like most Americans, Joan Blades is distressed by the hyperpartisan attack and counterattack that has characterized public life more and more. As a cofounder of MoveOn.org, which is known for taking progressive positions and raising money for progressive candidates, Blades knows partisanship firsthand. "When we create adversarial environments," she observes, "creative improvements become increasingly unlikely. Everything is a fight."

Blades first witnessed the dangerous consequences of dysfunctional relationship thirty years ago as a divorce mediator. "I saw firsthand how adversarial divorces were toxic for children," she recalls. "When parents made the effort to mediate their divorce agreement, the outcome was far better structured for both them and their children—and they were in a position to renegotiate as the children's needs changed. But if their relationship was angry and estranged, they would get stuck with obsolete agreements that did not work for anyone."

The same principles, she believes, apply to politics. When she witnessed American politics turning toxic and dysfunctional, she founded what she calls her own "domestic peace initiative": Living Room Conversations.[18] "I concluded that partisan lines had become so hardened that our capacity to solve problems had become dangerously impaired. I've become convinced that the only way we are going to be able to devise creative solutions responsive and flexible enough to meet the big challenges we face is by working collaboratively."

She cites the Affordable Care Act as a case in point. This health-care reform effort was a start, she says, "but only a start." Of course it needs continuous improvement, but "with Democrats in a defensive crouch and Republicans threatening to repeal, making it better is out of the question. It's just like a hostile divorce agreement: it ends up hurting everyone."

Fittingly, Living Room Conversations is a state-of-the-art method for individuals and organizations to bring both sides of the political spectrum together to discuss issues of interest in a comfortable environment. No facilitator is needed; the living room conversation simply needs guests and hosts to honor their six basic rules of discourse, which are remarkably similar to what the members of Congress adopted.

Living Room Conversation Ground Rules

BE CURIOUS AND OPEN TO LEARNING
Listen to and be open to hearing all points of view.
Maintain an attitude of exploration and learning.
Conversation is as much about listening as it is about talking.

SHOW RESPECT AND SUSPEND JUDGMENT
Human beings tend to judge one another; do your best not
to. Setting judgments aside will better enable you to learn
from others and help them feel respected and appreciated.

LOOK FOR COMMON GROUND
In this conversation, we look for what we agree on and
simply appreciate that we will disagree on some beliefs
and opinions.

BE AUTHENTIC AND WELCOME THAT FROM OTHERS
Share what's important to you. Speak authentically from
your personal and heartfelt experience. Be considerate to
others who are doing the same.

BE PURPOSEFUL AND TO THE POINT
Notice if what you are conveying is or is not "on purpose"
to the question at hand. Notice if you are making the same
point more than once.

OWN AND GUIDE THE CONVERSATION
Take responsibility for the quality of your participation
and the quality of the conversation by noticing what's
happening, and actively support getting yourself and
others back "on purpose" when needed.

"Based on my work as a grassroots organizer," Blades says,
"I believe that citizens are smart and caring, and when you en-

gage them, really substantial changes can happen. When we start talking to each other and listening to each other with respect, hearing each other's good ideas, there's an opportunity for us to create solutions that are dramatically better. I know that millions of people, when brought together, can build a more family-friendly America—if we work together as a transpartisan force, we can create a grassroots movement that turns this country around. I am looking for a snowball effect, and where better to start practicing that than in our own living rooms!"

Although we, the people, may not be able to immediately transform the White House, Capitol Hill, or our state legislatures into constructive, respectful problem-solving environments, Blades and her colleagues have proved that we can learn how to do so in our own neighborhoods.

Just as Joan Blades's venue is living rooms, Liz Joyner's is the community itself—specifically Tallahassee, Florida. Since 2006, she has devoted herself to inspiring transpartisan magic in Florida's state capital. Her project is simply called the Village Square, and its "secret sauce," as Joyner puts it, is informal get-togethers between conservatives and liberals, usually over a good meal. "If you want to get people together socially over civic issues," she says, "breaking bread really helps a lot."

The Village Square was born when a contentious local issue, fed by competing PR campaigns filled with half-truths and spin, divided Tallahassee. Joyner and her colleagues decided to bring the antagonists together to form an organization dedicated to honest conversation among neighbors. The result was that the dynamics of civic engagement changed and a movement was born. "The jostling of one opinion against the other is fundamental to our system of governance," she says. "The problem comes when we stop engaging to jostle." Having found the "secret sauce for how you do this," Joyner, like any good chef, aims to get in as many hands as possible.[19]

County Commissioner and Village Square cofounder Bryan Desloge, a longtime Republican, shares her enthusiasm. "Everybody's got different life experiences, and they bring those to the table," he observes. Participating in the Village Square "gets people back to the point of moving the agenda forward in a positive way. I think we've broken the code here and created something we can be proud of." The project has been so successful that sister organizations are springing up in several cities across the country.

A former Tallahassee City commissioner who led the Village Square's founding in Tallahassee, Allan Katz has launched the American Public Square in Kansas City, where he is now a political science professor. An ardent Democrat and major fundraiser for Barack Obama's 2008 campaign, Katz now firmly believes that political discourse has become so "awful" that it's just as important to build relationships between the sides as it is for his own side to win.

"For people who are not on the extremes, there is no place for them," says Katz. "The idea is to get the megaphone back to the people who aren't on the edges." As a father and grandfather, he feels that it's personal as well as political. "Our children have grown up in a world where the only thing they've seen is political dysfunction. Unless we change things, they're going to think this is normal. They need to understand there's another way."[20]

This other way is not rocket science. It is taking place every day in communities across America. The aptly named organization Everyday Democracy specializes in catalyzing and gathering examples of this other way in action.

The remarkable woman who leads Everyday Democracy, Martha McCoy, is part of this deliberative democracy movement, which is dedicated to deepening the way Americans talk and listen to each other. She has spent her life getting beyond the bland version of America broadcast by television in which citizens talk past one another and are left with stereotypes of each other. If one listens to McCoy's moving, down-to-earth stories of citizens finding their voice, one is inspired by the healing power of community-level engagement.[21]

"Let me describe what it tastes like," she says, when asked how Everyday Democracy operates. And then she tells the story of the Montgomery County school district, not far from Washington, DC, where educators were concerned about the achievement gap between white and minority students. "The great thing about democracy," she says, "is that experts aren't the only ones who know what's going on." As a result of a series of conversations involving the whole community, concrete changes in the functioning of the school system have helped reduce the gap so that all students feel better served.

The common denominator that unites the Public Conversations Project, Living Room Conversations, the Village Square, and Everyday Democracy is the priority they place on relationship. Just recall the essence of the new narrative that goes beyond partisanship:

> **Story #3:** Americans can work together with people different from ourselves to search for common ground that can strengthen the country that we all love.

That requires relationship—not drive-by debates, not attack-counterattack, and not photo ops with catchy one-liners. It requires sustained personal contact, preferably face-to-face, with genuine dialogue. *Relationship is a powerful catalyst for the kind of learning that transforms conflict into opportunity.*

Although applying this insight to political conflicts is not a new idea, the movement to reunite America is applying this old idea in new ways. The emphasis on respectful dialogue and relationship building with one's adversaries is as old as the Judeo-Christian tradition. Indeed, all major faiths share versions of the Golden Rule in their holy books. But what is new is the realization that these principles—advocated in churches, synagogues, and mosques around the world—cannot be limited to places of worship. These spiritual insights must respectfully enter the public square.

Fortunately, from both liberal and conservative origins, faith-based organizations are helping to bridge the partisan divide. There are scores of diverse religious organizations, ranging from the Faith and Politics Institute to the New Evangelical Partnership for the Common Good, which apply faith-based values to public issues in ways that unite rather than divide Americans against each other. The Institute's Doug Tanner speaks for many of his colleagues across the spectrum when he says their role is "evoking our better angels in politics."

Reverend Doug Tanner came to faith from a liberal background. A native of North Carolina, he is an ordained minister in the United Methodist Church who served as a campus chaplain, a parish minister, a congressional aide, and a political campaign consultant before helping to found the Faith and Politics Institute, which holds regular prayer meetings for members of Congress as well as organizing cross-party learning journeys. Despite the liberal origins of the Faith and Politics Institute, there is nothing in its views that would repel conservative Christians—as long they have an open mind.

Even those who have a deep devotion to Christianity, Judaism, Islam, or another faith tradition recognize that their relationship to the civic and ecological fabric also deserves their devotion. In 2008, after twenty-eight years working for the National Association of Evangelicals, Richard Cizik resigned as the organization's vice president for governmental affairs. Despite his conservative credentials, his evolving views on same-sex marriage and climate change put him at odds with his hard-line colleagues, leading the Association's president to cite a "loss of trust" in him as their spokesperson."[22] But if one listens to Cizik closely and learns about the positions of his New Evangelical Partnership, one does not find him untrustworthy at all. He is a man of God who accepts Jesus as his savior and who is committed to continuing to deepen his relationship to the earth, the divine, and his fellow Americans of all faiths.[23]

In every sector of society, then, relationship matters. Reuniting the country actually depends on it. Of course, pragmatic political operatives will argue that it is the number of votes that actually matters. But practical dealmakers in Washington, DC, know that, in fact, relationships are fundamental to real long-term change.

Michael Ostrolenk, the libertarian founder of the Liberty Coalition, whom we met in chapter 1, built his ninety-four-organization coalition by focusing on this key ingredient. MoveOn.org, Americans for Tax Reform, and the ACLU participate in the Liberty Coalition because they share similar concerns about the Patriot Act and intrusions into our civil liberties. But Ostrolenk's more enduring purpose for the Coalition was that he "wanted to create relationships across the spectrum that would survive over time." It has taken Ostrolenk and his colleagues more than a decade of hard work, but, he says proudly, "it's finally happening."[24]

In the long run, relationship between adversaries matters more than which adversary wins. From a partisan perspective, victory is sweet. But from a patriotic perspective, two parties working together are better than one party dominating. "Two are better off than one," the Holy Bible says, "because together they can work more effectively." If one stumbles, the Scripture explains, the other can offer support. If they are attacked, they can defend themselves better than either of them alone.[25]

This ancient message from Ecclesiastes still rings true in the political life of America today. Two parties are better than one. They are a godsend—as long as they work together to strengthen the country that they both love.

THREE

CHAMPIONING
THE WHOLE TRUTH

*From Position Taking
to Problem Solving*

THE DANGER

Taking positions so rigidly that we undermine trust and prevent innovation.

THE OPPORTUNITY

Solving problems by learning with, and relating to, our adversaries so that together we discover new opportunities.

SUMMARY

Moving from control to relationship changes the very dynamics of politics. Solving a problem, then, is more highly valued than simply holding a position. Ensuring that all voices are heard before decisions are made—not just the predictable polarized extremes—becomes a higher priority. After too many years of dead-end, hard-line position taking, both citizens and candidates are clamoring for something different: not position taking, but problem solving.

SPOTLIGHT ON

Aakif Ahmad, Rob Fersh, Newt Gingrich, Van Jones, Nancy Jacobson, Steven Kull, Dini Merz, Mark McKinnon, Grover Norquist, Richard Parsons, Ron Shaich, Bill Shireman, Marvin Smith, and the participants in the "Defending America, Defending Taxpayers" retreat.

THE DANGER
Positions Set in Stone

IN 2007, at a retreat designed to promote greater cross-party dialogue between members from opposing parties, the chiefs of staff from the US House of Representatives and Senate made remarkable progress thinking through some highly charged legislative issues and finding promising areas of agreement. Toward the close of the retreat, one chief of staff pulled me aside. "If this process gets any traction," he said in a hushed voice, "both our parties' leaders will squash it like a bug."

This chief of staff witnessed firsthand that if a breakthrough idea was achieved through genuine collaboration with "them," the House speaker or minority leader would kill it before it reached the House or Senate floor.

Because we humans, consciously or unconsciously, tend to slant information to suit our self-interest, the law requires that witnesses who take the stand in a court of law pledge that they will "speak the truth, the whole truth, and nothing but the truth." Voters, candidates, and political consultants, however, are never asked to make such a vow. So in politics, it is common for all concerned to manipulate the truth to support their position.

It is healthy for citizens to take positions on issues. After all, this is how decisions are made in a democracy. Officials ask a question and expect us to answer:

> Should the school board close an elementary school in order to save money?
>
> Yes ☐   No ☐

Do you support an increase in gasoline taxes to fund
infrastructure repair?

Yes ☐   No ☐

This kind of yes-no, pro-con position taking is the meat and po-
tatoes of political discourse. It is the heart of debate—and debate
has been the benchmark of democracy. One takes a position,
or a side, and argues for it passionately. One's opponents take
a sharply contrasting position, and the other side promotes it
with equal vigor. Healthy democracy rests on the premise that
the side with the strongest position will win.

But as we have seen, the corrosive impact of hyperpartisan
politics can distort what is healthy about democracy and make
it toxic. This is precisely what has happened to debate-driven
position taking. Rather than encouraging careful consideration
of complex current issues, hyperpartisan politics forces hard-
and-fast pro-or-con position taking. Instead of leaders who
take a fresh look at tough issues, we have leaders stuck in stale,
diametrically opposed positions. Whether the issue is climate
change, immigration, or gun rights doesn't matter. The subtext
is always the same: my position versus your position until hell
freezes over.

Climate Change

There is no commentary in the founding documents of our
country about this issue because the Founding Fathers did not,
even in their wildest dreams, consider the North American climate relevant to political debate. They considered the temperature of the air, the tides of the sea, and the rays of the sun to be
God's work, not ours.

Yet now candidates for national office must wrestle with
this intensely partisan issue. Gone is the time when the Clean

Air Act of 1970 passed the Senate on a bipartisan vote of 73 to 0 and then was signed into law by President Richard Nixon. Today, when the Environmental Protection Agency proposes regulations to curb emissions of health-impairing ozone, it becomes yet another left-right showdown. Aspiring politicians get the message that they had better take a position on climate change—and quickly. Even if you are the son of a governor and the grandson of a president, you can expect a hyperpartisan attack if you have the courage to think for yourself.

In 2014, George P. Bush, the son of former Florida Governor Jeb Bush, ran for land commissioner in Texas. It seemed like a low-profile, low-risk entry position that could launch his political career. But that was before he dared to say what was on his mind.

In an interview, the young Bush openly shared his belief that climate change is a serious threat to Texas and that the state should "transition to a natural gas–based energy economy and then, in the long term, renewables." The increased vulnerability of Texas's 367-mile Gulf Coast to hurricanes, sea-level rise, and coastal erosion, he said, "honestly keeps me up at night."

That angered many Texas Tea Party activists. Because he had opposed abortion, attacked the Affordable Care Act, and promoted gun rights, they thought that this new-generation member of America's leading Republican family would be their champion. But when he spoke his mind about climate change, he deviated from the party line. Allison DeFoor, who had served as an environmental adviser to his father, Jeb, explained George P.'s courage this way: "I can just tell you that I would be surprised if the fruit fell very far from the tree, and the tree here is data driven."

Obliged to justify his views, George P. said, "From Day 1 . . . I was always going to run based on my principles."[1]

The same pressure to conform on the right, it seems, awaits those who do not conform on the left. Michael Shellenberger and Ted Nordhaus, two scholars with solid liberal credentials, launched the Breakthrough Institute because they wanted to produce policy recommendations on energy and climate based on science, not ideology. But then they began to question well-known environmentalists' pronouncements about the miraculous benefits of solar power and renewable energy. Even more offensive to some environmentalists, they began to argue in favor of nuclear energy as a necessary power source for America. If our country truly intends to reduce our reliance on high-polluting coal, they believe, we will need nuclear power—whether we like it or not.

According to these two men, their failure to subscribe to liberal orthodoxy has made them a target for "climate McCarthyism." They bitterly complain that their progressive critics are more interested in advancing the candidates and ideology of the Democratic Party than in the actual facts of climate change.[2] In this kind of hostile environment, accusation replaces inquiry—and policy making suffers.

Taken to its extreme, this kind of position taking becomes nothing more than the verbal equivalent of a street fight. It's all about knocking out your opponent. If hyperpartisans can turn even a science-based issue like climate change into an attack–counterattack battlefield, just imagine what it can do with issues that are profoundly value based, such as immigration and gun control policy.

Immigration

Imagine for a moment that you are a candidate at a campaign stop and a voter asks you about your views on immigration. The lives of many families, and the spirit and integrity of our country, hinge on the outcome of this debate. But does the debate do justice to the complexity of the issue?

You know your party's position on the issue. You have been coached about what to say, and not to say, and on the importance of sticking to your talking points and keeping it simple. If you are in a heavily conservative district running as a Republican, you have your pitch. ("Build a wall!") Similarly, if you are a Democrat running in a liberal district, you have your lines memorized. ("We are all immigrants!") As a candidate, you are prepared—you know what position you are taking, and you can articulate it clearly and compellingly. But does your position actually have anything to do with doing what's best for America?

"You can't deport eleven million people—so what do we do?" asks Al Cardenas, the former president of the American Conservative Union, who is both a former chairman of the Florida Republican Party and a Cuban immigrant. "How many visas do we issue? How many are given to high-skilled entrepreneurs who want to start businesses that will create jobs? How many go to poor low-skilled refugees running away from violence and seeking asylum?" And if the economic dimension alone is not confusing enough, Cardenas overlays the humanitarian dimension. "We believe in reunifying families. But what is family? Is it only parents and children . . . or also brothers and sisters . . . or also siblings' families?"

Like immigration, most issues facing America in the 2016 elections are not ones that can be resolved by knee-jerk, uninformed position taking. The danger of hyperpartisans is that, instead of asking tough questions as Cardenas advocates, we will be served simplistic pro-versus-con positions. We will not witness a fair and thorough exploration of the issue. Instead, we will be offered a toxic form of political position taking that exploits people's fears, terrifies undocumented immigrants and their children, and leaves the nation even further adrift and divided.

Gun Policy

What is alarming is that hyperpartisan position taking continues to rule the day even when lives are at stake.

With grief for the murdered kindergartners still fresh, the tragic school massacre in Newtown, Connecticut, offered an opportunity for genuine problem solving. Most Americans were aghast that someone, even suffering mental illness, would target five-year-olds and their teachers. We were also startled into recognizing how defenseless our elementary schools were. Instead, the same old positions were soon pitted against each other. Within days of the mass shooting, two camps began vying to control the debate. On one side, there were those who felt that the massacre at Sandy Hook Elementary School (and the many mass shootings that have followed since then) proved once and for all the need for stricter gun control. On the other side, there were those who considered it proof positive that we need more guns throughout our society. As the participants in one debate summarized it:

NO ON GUN CONTROL

"Gun restrictions leave people vulnerable
and helpless."

–JOHN LOTT, AUTHOR, *MORE GUNS, LESS CRIME*

"Teachers should be allowed to carry firearms."

–GENE HOFFMAN, CHAIRMAN,
CALGUNS FOUNDATION

"Stricter gun control laws will only make
citizens less safe."

—ERICH PRATT, DIRECTOR OF COMMUNICATIONS,
GUN OWNERS OF AMERICA

YES ON GUN CONTROL

"Obama and Congress must seize the opportunity
to curb gun violence."

—JOSHUA HORWITZ, EXECUTIVE DIRECTOR,
COALITION TO STOP GUN VIOLENCE

"Gun control policies should be strengthened,
but not haphazardly."

—JOHN HUDAK, FELLOW, BROOKINGS INSTITUTION

"Parents should not have to doubt
their children are safe at school."

—KRISTIN ROWE-FINKBEINER, CEO, MOMSRISING

As the magazine that hosted the debate observed, the argument became even more heated after the shocking mass murder than it was before. On the one hand, ten states went on to pass legislation permitting teachers and school officials to arm themselves in order to prevent further mass shootings. On the other hand, two teachers in the span of two weeks accidentally shot themselves at school. This supported the gun control argument that having more guns in classrooms was not part of the solution but actually put schoolchildren in greater danger.

If killing twenty children and six school staff members doesn't break through our ideological "twin spin" machines, what will? More partisan position taking simply means that school children in the future will be just as endangered as

they were before Sandy Hook. Today, mentally ill mass mur-
derers can still get a gun and attack any elementary school in
America. Guns will continue to be accessible to any aggressive
sociopathic who wants to kill postal workers, fellow soldiers,
Jews, women, blacks, kindergartners, moviegoers, news reporters, or whomever the target of their insane rage may be.
We have to develop a national a policy that respects both arguments: (1) We cannot leave schools defenseless and hope for
the best; and (2) every principal, teacher, school playground
supervisor, and school bus driver in America cannot be required to wear a gun on his or her hip.

★

As climate change, immigration, and gun policy illustrate, the
danger of superpolarized position taking should be crystal
clear. A country divided by simplistic, polarized "yes" and "no"
will do nothing. No national unity can emerge if we, the people,
are given only divisive alternatives. Just imagine if President
Kennedy had polled the American people with pro-or-con
choices about going to the moon. We would never have gotten
off the launching pad!

If one stuck position creates rigidity, two competing stuck
positions build in divisiveness. I attended a meeting recently in
Washington, DC, in which participants were polled on energy
and global warming. Respondents had to choose between (a)
having government "take no action" and (b) having government "interfere" in the market. These are choices designed to
polarize. The obvious common-sense answer was a nonexis-
tent option (c): government and business should work together
to meet this challenge facing our country and the world. But
no one could check option (c), much less the option "I don't
know," because they were not given the choice.

Hyperpartisan polarized choices are making our country resemble a car with two warring drivers, the Democratic Party and the Republican Party, who are fighting for control over the steering wheel. As the engine that fuels America sputters, misfires, and repeatedly underperforms, both drivers ignore the warning signs and just keep on fighting for the steering wheel. Whoever gets the momentary advantage grabs it, turns the car to the left or the right, and hits the accelerator. Meanwhile, the other driver tries to slam on the brakes and flip it around. America is an accident waiting to happen.

Although many Republicans and Democrats, as individuals, know how to play the role of bipartisan bridge builder, the locked-in partisan polarization of the two-party system turns the aisle between the parties into a chasm. This dividing line often makes moderate leaders on both sides of the aisle feel powerless. Privately, members from both sides of the House of Representatives resent that their respective party leaders dominate the proceedings to such an extent that they lose their voice.

Even members of the majority party feel disenfranchised by the two-sided straitjacket. "You don't seem to understand," one of the most respected and well-placed Republican representatives confided to me once, "I am powerless!" Although the House was under Republican control at the time, this senior lawmaker felt so disempowered by the party leadership that he felt he could make no difference. Because of this partisan stranglehold on the institution, bipartisan collaboration is virtually extinct.

This is the partisan danger: a superpower paralyzed, defeated not by a foreign army but by two parties quarreling incessantly about their competing fragments of the truth.

THE OPPORTUNITY
Innovating through Collaboration

For the past several decades, the American prison population has skyrocketed. All the while, our elected leaders have been unable to stop the ridiculously inefficient and astronomically expensive trend that has put nonviolent offenders behind bars for decades. What finally triggered widespread public concern was the collaboration of two unlikely allies: archconservative former Republican Speaker of the House Newt Gingrich and ultraliberal ex-Obama appointee Van Jones. Together, these two tough-minded partisans joined together to promote the cross-partisan initiative #Cut50, designed to reduce the prison population by 50 percent.[3]

Having worked side by side as CNN commentators, the two men became friends. They discovered that, like others on the right and left, they shared some basic concerns about America. Through a process of dialogue and mutual learning, they found themselves committed to the same cause: putting "justice" back into the criminal justice system. For different reasons, they wanted to challenge a system that cost $80 billion annually to keep two million people behind bars.

"Putting a juvenile delinquent in a detention center costs $90,000 a year," says Gingrich. "You could send them to Harvard, Yale, or Stanford for dramatically less money! As long as they aren't a violent or hardened criminal, putting them in that detention center for a first offense may make them less likely to have a decent future."

From Van Jones's perspective, the right deserves a lot of credit for evolving on this critical issue. He sees three conservative constituencies all moving toward problem solving for their own reasons: (1) "evangelical Christians concerned about each human soul," (2) "fiscal conservatives concerned about high taxes to pay for prisons," and (3) "libertarians concerned about freedom" and limiting the power of the state. The result: a handful of bills already introduced into Congress. Without a doubt, Jones believes, "criminal justice reform will be one of the major bipartisan breakthroughs in many, many years in Washington, DC."

Together the two men hosted a cross-spectrum summit on this issue that was attended by a stellar cast of liberal and conservative supporters, including former Attorney General Eric Holder and representatives from the Koch brothers. "You'd never have thought you'd see the Obama cabinet and the Koch brothers in the same room!" exclaims Jones with pride. "When you meet in the middle, there are some issues that just pop right up!"

In fact, criminal justice reform did not just "pop right up." The success of #cut50, which was founded by Matt Haney and Jessica Jackson, was the result of the work of many transpartisan pioneers who had been fertilizing the transpartisan soil together for years. Grover Norquist, president of Americans for Tax Reform, and Joan Blades, founder of MoveOn.org, had already worked together to build a bridge across the partisan divide that made the issue "safe" for bipartisan collaboration. This helped to catalyze the founding of the Coalition for Public Safety, which was the brainchild of a remarkable cross-section of organizations ranging from the Center for American Progress on the left to Koch Industries on the right. A few months later, Van Jones cohosted an event for Blades's Living Room Conversations project, where he shared details about his new partnership with Gingrich to promote #Cut50.[4]

It was no coincidence that candidates for the 2016 presidential election from both ends of the political spectrum began promoting reform of the criminal justice system. It had become safe enough to cross the partisan divide because these coura- geous pathfinders had shown the way. They had put the new narrative—Americans can work together with people different from ourselves to search for common ground—into action.

That search, if successful, will lead to hundreds of thou- sands of lives reclaimed, tens of billions of dollars saved, and a renewal of our criminal justice system.

Enduring coalitions across the divides take hard work and the capacity to manage complex relationships among adversar- ies who are being constantly pulled apart by their competing constituencies. Fortunately, a new generation of bridge build- ers is emerging who are making the reuniting of America their full-time mission.

Marvin Smith, a millennial-generation African American, works with Future 500, a pioneering business-based organiza- tion that serves as a bridge across the divide that often sepa- rates corporations from their critics. As manager of stakeholder engagement, Smith is responsible for doing what would have once seemed impossible. His job is to bring together people who, as he puts it, "typically love to hate each other."

"I have lived my life through a transpartisan lens," he says matter-of-factly. "I did so without knowing that there was a growing community and movement of people who were doing the same thing."

What makes him transpartisan, Smith says, is that he has "seen the potential for innovative impact that goes far beyond the competing left–right mindsets.

"What we have realized is that NGO [nongovernmental or- ganization] purpose and corporate power, when aligned, can achieve broad systemic change. When we come into a tense, conflicted situation, our first step is to understand the positions

CHAMPIONING THE WHOLE TRUTH

people are taking in their firmly held beliefs. True stakeholder engagement begins with respecting and identifying positions and then searching for common ground. We go to each side and reassure them that we hear them and care about their beliefs. We ask: Why do you feel this way? What leads to your passion and enthusiasm?

"Then," Smith says, "we can shift into real problem solving." It is not about waiting to see if diverse stakeholders get involved. It is about actively identifying, recruiting, and facilitating a wide spectrum of viewpoints to design breakthrough approaches to difficult issues.

No one is more eloquent about how to catalyze and harness problem solving than the self-described "transpartisan Republican" founder of Future 500, Bill Shireman. As an entrepreneur himself, he believes in certain core conservative premises but knows that working across the spectrum is often the best way to reach one's goals.

Case in point: the economy.

"Conservatives are right: as a nation, we are out of money and deep in debt," says Shireman in the opening of his "new agenda for America." But then he quickly adds: "Progressives are also right: we can't pay off our debt by extracting it from the poor, the middle class, or the environment."

As part of his new agenda, Shireman goes on to outline dozens of initiatives to "bridge the left and the right and move America forward."[5] Future 500 is working hard across the political spectrum to build alliances between formerly adversarial stakeholders on issues such as energy and climate change, food and water, materials and supply chains, and other pressing policy issues. Shireman is part of a wave of businesspeople that is providing momentum for candidates who refuse to play the left-versus-right game with economic issues.

Riding that wave is Ron Shaich, the founder and CEO of the St. Louis-based retail food chain Panera Bread, who volunteered a few years ago to go hungry for a week. He committed himself to meet the "SNAP challenge." The Supplemental Nutrition Assistance Program (SNAP), formerly known as the food stamp program, challenges volunteers and supporters to live on a food and beverage budget of $4.50 a day for one week. That is the amount awarded to food stamp recipients.

"I thought I knew a thing or two about hunger," Shaich, a lifelong Republican who is now active in No Labels, told a CNN reporter. "I've met thousands of people who struggle to feed themselves and their families; visited dozens of soup kitchens, food pantries, homeless shelters, and food banks; and worked closely with nonprofit organizations in trying to find new ways to end hunger. I really thought I understood the scope of the problem. But let me tell you something—I had no clue."

His approach to the challenge was to buy foods that were filling and cheap, which meant mostly carbohydrates. "Fresh fruit, vegetables, and yogurt were too expensive. I also gave up coffee because it didn't fit the budget. I only drank water."

Shaich admits that doing this for a week was just a temporary imitation of the real experience of poverty. But it taught him that hunger is too serious an issue to be turned into a political football. And it helped him publicize to his fellow businesspeople and fellow conservatives that hunger is "not about them, but about us."

His message couldn't be clearer: a more innovative economic approach beyond the stock answer of the polarized parties is needed. "You don't stay CEO of a company for very long if you don't solve problems," he often says. "And if you don't solve problems, you get fired."

One organization in Washington, DC, that is committed to cross-spectrum problem solving is the Convergence Center for Policy Resolution. It has managed to tackle several of the thorniest partisan controversies with significant success and without aligning itself with either Democrats or Republicans. As Aakif Ahmad, Convergence cofounder and chief operating officer, explains, the organization was founded to answer one simple yet powerful question: "Are there other better ways to create change than each of us pushing our own agendas as hard as we can?"

The answer, he believes, is a clear yes. "There *are* antidotes to gridlock," he argues, if four practices are followed: (1) creating a safe space for dialogue, (2) building on an agreed-upon framework, (3) promoting trust and understanding, and (4) ensuring diverse participation. Considering the wide range of issues that Convergence has worked on—education, nutrition, poverty, long-term care, and others—Ahmad concludes that "no one person or perspective holds all the answers. Better, stronger, and more lasting solutions can emerge if we foster more communication and more cooperation among those that disagree."[6]

Not surprisingly, the original impetus to establish Convergence grew out of its founder's experience as a staffer on Capitol Hill. "I kept meeting very decent people who sincerely wanted to solve problems but who saw the world differently than I did," recalls Rob Fersh, president of Convergence. "The system was set up for me to debate them and win the argument, not solve a problem. But I noticed that they often made good points. What struck me was that we needed a place to really talk and understand each other so we could find answers that were better than what any of us started with. But on the Hill that just wasn't possible."

With Ahmad, Fersh started Convergence to fill that gap. With a board as diverse as America itself, "we continue to disagree on policy but are united in the power of dialogue," he says. In their "dialogue leading to action," they have seen that opposing views often find more common ground than they initially imagined.

The bridge-building efforts of organizations like Convergence and Future 500 may seem futile in a country that appears so hopelessly divided. But is the country really so divided—or is it just the two parties that are?

One public opinion expert who is also not working for the Democrats or Republicans believes that, in fact, a deep current of agreement flows beneath the well-publicized divide. Steven Kull, founder of Voice of the People, led a study that found dramatically less difference between the views of people who live in red and blue districts or states than one would imagine. The study, detailed in their report *A Not So Divided America*, found that comparing the policy positions of people who live in red districts and blue districts reveals that in the vast majority of issues, they agree.

- On only 4 percent of the questions (14 out of 388) did a majority or plurality of those living in red congressional districts/states disagree with the majority or plurality in the blue districts/states.

- For a large majority of questions—69 percent—(266 of 388), there were no statistically significant differences between the views in the red districts/states and the blue districts/states.[7]

The bridge-building opportunity here is breathtaking: there is an invisible America that is ready for problem solving, but it is hidden by a visible, party-driven America that is ad-dicted to position taking.

"The fact is, Americans are more united than divided," says Richard Parsons, executive director, Voice of the People. "Giving the people a greater voice would help break the gridlock in Washington." Or, as Kull pointedly concludes: "If you ask them to choose between two competing slogans like 'Government regulation does more harm than good' or 'The government needs to do more,' people are more polarized. But when you ask them specific policy questions about what the government should do, the number of issues on which Republicans and Democrats differ is relatively small. When people have an op-portunity to think and deliberate, they tend to move toward more common-ground positions."

The key ingredients in problem solving are sticking to the facts and speaking the truth, as best we know it. Fortunately, in the nation's capital, a new generation of nonprofit organi-zations has emerged whose advocacy agenda is simple: truth telling. Although everything inside the Washington Beltway in-volves some spin, these organizations—with names like Truth in Government and the Coalition for Evidence-Based Policy—are primarily pushing facts and figures. They are so concerned about political spinning that they have become lobbyists for the truth.

But if we think problem solving across the divides is easy, we had better think twice. It is very hard to do in private, and even harder in public. I was fortunate to have the privilege of fa-cilitating a pioneering retreat a few years ago called "Defending America, Defending Taxpayers," which dramatically illustrated that it is possible to achieve remarkable consensus on tough is-sues but challenging to sustain it in the public eye.

This meeting included more than two dozen participating organizations, spanning the political spectrum, that gathered to address the threat of our runaway defense budget.[8] Because our misshapen defense budget is so disturbing, this remarkable cross-section of concerned citizens included very "conservative" representatives of Tea Party affiliates and very "progressive" peace-oriented groups, as well as think tanks from the left and right.

This meeting also included an Army colonel who is very familiar with Pentagon procurement practices; he told the participants in the bluntest terms possible, "We need a *threat*-based defense budget. What we have now is a *contractor*-based defense budget. It's putting our nation and our troops at risk!"

The colonel pointed out that the Department of Defense budget has ballooned, inflated by both our fears of terrorism and the wasteful contracting system. Even former Secretary of Defense Robert Gates has condemned the "gusher of defense spending" that opened up after the September 11 attacks. In a speech at the Eisenhower Library, he asserted that a huge number of generals and admirals are feeding at the trough of federal military spending and creating a layer of bureaucracy so thick and so wasteful that military operations are doomed to inefficiency and redundancy. After World War II, war production shifted back to focusing on producing nonmilitary goods. Now, Gates said, the armaments industry has become a permanent fixture of our economy.

> Does the number of warships we have, and are building, really put America at risk, when the U.S. battle fleet is larger than the next 13 navies combined—11 of which are our partners and allies? Is it a dire threat that by 2020, the United States will have only 20 times more advanced stealth fighters than China? These are the kinds of questions Eisenhower asked as commander in chief. They are the kinds of questions I believe he would ask today.[9]

Presidents from Madison to Eisenhower and now even secretaries of defense are warning us not to keep throwing away
our money. As one of the leading Senate conservatives, Tom
Coburn (R-Oklahoma), has said: "Our nation's $16 trillion
national debt is the new red menace, posing perhaps a greater
threat to our nation than any other military adversary."[10]

Inspired by the challenge of meeting this threat to American
security, these more than two dozen committed policy experts
worked around the clock for more than two days to come to an
agreement about how to work together in spending the gargan-
tuan sum of national defense money more wisely.

After some tough debate and hard negotiating, the participants put aside their preconceived ideologies, tabled other
issues on which they vehemently disagreed, and found a remarkable degree of consensus. They agreed on principles that
would reduce the size of the defense budget (and our debt!) and
at the same time increase our national security. On the closing
morning, the participants were both amazed and proud. They
had reached consensus and committed to working together behind the scenes to apply liberal-conservative pressure toward
reshaping the Pentagon budget so that it would be less wasteful—and more effective.

"It's very hard to hate someone who you sit with face to
face. Even if someone's values differ from my own, if they are
sincerely held, I can connect with them as a person. . . . What
came out of that meeting are partnerships that, even to this
day, are growing," says Dini Merz, director of the Colombe
Foundation, which launched and sustains the Pentagon Budget
Campaign and helped to organize the gathering.

We have made over $4 million in grants to organiza-
tions on all sides to work with their constituencies to

promote the idea that we can cut $100 billion a year
from the Pentagon budget for the next ten years without hurting our national security. These strands of partnership are just getting stronger and stronger because
people know each other and are starting to like each
other. Their work has created space for decision makers and elected officials to make reasoned stands on
the Pentagon budget without fear of attacks for being
weak on defense. On subjects like Pentagon spending
and criminal justice reform, it seems that people are
realizing that *we can work together on an issue without
agreeing on everything!*

The Pentagon Budget Campaign uses legislative, communications, and field-building tactics to help members sustain their
alliances and work together to foster more nuanced debate on
responsibly reducing the size of the Pentagon budget through
legislative, communications, and field-building efforts. Every
time an organization takes a public stand, the Pentagon Budget
Campaign helps to get as many cosigners as possible from both
sides of the aisle. Because of the Campaign, congressional staff-
ers from all sides of the political spectrum have formed ties that
are creating across-the-aisle dialogue to bring more common-
sense approaches to defense-spending appropriations.

Whether it is the Pentagon Budget Campaign,
Convergence, Future 500, or #Cut50, all have shifted from
position taking to problem solving by moving beyond ster-
ile debate and engaging in genuine dialogue. The difference
between the two processes could not be more profound.
Healthy, honest debate is a first-rate tool for deciding between
two options. But it is a lousy, ineffective tool for creating a better option. If two sides are debating second-rate proposals, the
debate itself cannot generate a better one. Dialogue, however,

is designed for precisely this purpose. It is a process not only of advocacy but also of inquiry. It is about discovering, for example, if the advantages of polarized Positions A and B can be integrated into an innovative Position C.

Debate-Dialogue Chart[11]

DEBATE	DIALOGUE
Assume that you/your party is always right.	Open to the possibility that many people/parties have parts of the answer.
Combative: proving the other side wrong.	Collaborative: participants work together toward common understanding.
Listening to find flaws and rebut arguments.	Listening to understand, find meaning, and reach agreement.
Defending our own assumptions as truth.	Revealing our assumptions for re-evaluation.
Seeing only two sides.	Seeing all sides of an issue.
Defending one's own views against others.	Admitting that others' thinking can improve on one's own.
Searching for weaknesses in others' positions.	Searching for strengths and value in others' positions.
Creating a winner and loser.	Keeping the topic open in order to generate new possibilities.
Seeking a conclusion that supports your position.	Discovering new options that are more innovative and synergistic than the original alternatives.

While the projects highlighted so far in this chapter are fostering dialogue-based problem solving from outside government, others are trying to foster it from the inside. Thanks to its two visionary leaders, Republican Mark McKinnon and Democrat Nancy Jacobson, No Labels is promoting exactly this process in the United States Congress. Under their leadership, No Labels gathered more than ninety members of the US House of Representatives into a "problem-solving caucus." After great deliberation and polling, these legislators set a cross-party agenda that attempts to fill the vacuum with agreed-upon goals for the nation. "No Labels is calling for a National Strategic Agenda organized around goals that are widely shared across partisan and ideological lines," explains McKinnon, who served as chief media adviser for both George W. Bush and John McCain. By carefully polling both politicians and citizens, No Labels is promoting a national agenda that has earned strong support from both sides of the aisle.

"A big part of the problem," says McKinnon, "is that we don't even have any agreed-upon national goals, something most competitive nations have clearly established. Once goals are agreed upon, you can debate about how best to achieve them. But without goals, any enterprise is destined to drift or, worse, not move at all . . . which seems an adequate description for where we are today."

When confronted with the predictable attacks from the right ("You're just liberals in camouflage!") and the left ("You're just cozying up to the Tea Party crazies!"), McKinnon does not flinch. For example, he was once asked about Rush Limbaugh's accusation that No Labels consisted of liberals and progressives in masquerade. When progressives felt that their philosophy was being rejected by the American people, Limbaugh argued, they simply started "calling themselves the No Labels group."

"Well, I'm delighted that we got Rush Limbaugh's attention," responded McKinnon. "I am a Republican and a proud

Republican, as are many of our members. But we are not about ideology; we are about working together. Rush Limbaugh doesn't have any interest in people working together, so I'm not surprised he would attack us."[12]

Why would anyone attack problem solving? The answer is simple: problem solving threatens hyperpartisans. If someone on the left or right is committed to a worldview of good (us) and evil (them), collaboration is upsetting. Hyperpartisans want to erect a fence between good and evil and then persuade everyone to come over to their side. It is a great strategy for manipulative campaigning. But it is a lousy strategy for governing a complex, diverse twenty-first-century democracy like America.

Thanks to visionary leaders such as those profiled in this chapter, problem solving is gaining ground at every level of decision making—even Capitol Hill. Inch by inch, issue by issue, our fellow citizens are rolling up their sleeves and "working together across differences to find common ground that can strengthen the country that we all love."

FOUR

SERVING THE PEOPLE

*From Endless Campaigning
to Public Service*

THE DANGER

Campaigning that reduces every issue to a struggle for power between competing extremes who continue battling with each other long after the election is over.

THE OPPORTUNITY

Campaigning for a healthy, time-limited period to select leaders who will truly serve the best interests of the public.

SUMMARY

Whether or not one wants a smaller government, we all want an effective government. The term *public service*, which now seems almost antiquated, stands for a noble yet humble attitude that puts the quest for power and victory second, and the genuine desire to serve the people first. The change agents in this chapter are working from the grassroots to state legislatures, from living rooms to Capitol Hill, to make public service a reality.

SPOTLIGHT ON

Jon Avlon, David Burstein, Ted Celeste, Representative John K. Delaney, Representative Tom Cole, Representative Mickey Edwards, Jason Grumet, Walter Isaacson, Linda Killian, Carolyn Lukensmeyer, David Nevins, Amanda Kathryn Roman, and Jackie Salit.

THE DANGER

Trapped in a Downward Spiral

POLITICAL CAMPAIGNS were originally designed to make governing more responsive to the people and effective in its operations. But when partisanship becomes too extreme, the opposite occurs: governing becomes less responsive and less effective. In fact, public service dies.

During the twenty-first-century Bush and Obama administrations, the divide between the two major parties dramatically widened. While the gap in values on other dimensions (gender, age, race, class, etc.) stayed relatively stable, party affiliation split the nation apart more dramatically than at any point in the past generation.[1]

Nowhere did this fissure in the heart of America reveal itself more clearly than in campaigning and governing. Campaigns became more divisive and bitter, and governing became more chaotic and ineffectual. Democrats, behind closed doors, did everything they could to stop George W. Bush from succeeding; Republicans, even more outspokenly, committed themselves to blocking any initiative from Barack Obama.[2]

"The single most important thing we want to achieve," said Senate Minority Leader Mitch McConnell during the 2012 election, "is for President Obama to be a one-term president." Meanwhile, Vice President Joe Biden has said that he spoke with seven Republican senators who, according to Biden, were pressured by McConnell to be unified in their opposition to anything the Democrats proposed. The Republican senators told Biden, "Joe, we can't help you on *anything*. For the next two years, we can't let you succeed on anything. That's our ticket to coming back."[3]

The Republicans' strategy of undermining Obama proved effective. Like his predecessor President George W. Bush, Obama has lamented his inability to lead in the face of hyper-partisan opposition on everything. "The election is over—we're not competing anymore," pleaded President Obama in a 2010 meeting, as he sought the support of Senator John McCain and other legislators for the Affordable Care Act. Obama was trying to convince them that his 2008 election meant that campaigning should give way to governing. But he discovered, as had Bush, that today the toxic partisanship of ever-longer campaigns is not over on Election Day. In fact, it never ends.[4]

Unless something changes, the future inhabitants of 1600 Pennsylvania Avenue will discover themselves trapped in the same hyperpartisan straitjacket. Before our leaders will change, we first have to change the rules of the game.

As any avid sports fan knows, the rules matter. They profoundly affect the quality, and often the outcome, of the game.

When sports fans watch the Super Bowl, the World Series, the NCAA finals, or the World Cup, we know what's fair and what's not. That is because, as a culture, we have learned how to set up a competition between two teams and conduct a tough but fair contest that inspires both the players and the fans. Our major sporting events are, by and large, officiated fairly and organized efficiently, with clear and transparent outcomes. Fans accept the outcome, leave the stadium without rancor, and (perhaps after celebrating or commiserating over a beer) go home. Because the game is usually played fairly, the fans stay enthusiastically involved.

In politics, however, we have not done nearly as good a job. Instead of neutral referees or umpires, we have partisan secretaries of state. Instead of a neutral convener like the NFL or NCAA, we have the party-dominated Federal Election

Commission. And instead of clear, enforceable rules, we have a chaotic hodgepodge of regulations that are often ignored, violated, and rarely enforced. These are not design failures. These are direct consequences of the hyperpartisan epidemic.

To understand how the movement to reunite America is strengthening governance in America, let us contrast the forces that are undermining our country with the steps that our fellow citizens are taking to reunite America.

From Dividing to Uniting America

DIVIDING AMERICA	REUNITING AMERICA
1. Civic disengagement	1. Dynamic citizen engagement
2. Divided state legislatures	2. Collaborative state legislatures
3. Partisan election officials	3. Trustworthy elections
4. Endless campaigns	4. Inspiring campaigns
5. Broken governance	5. Effective governance

Civic Disengagement

As the hyperpartisan poison takes hold of the body politic, voters disconnect from the system in order to protect themselves. To put it bluntly, we give up—or we get angry.

> Since they've allowed all the money in politics, it's gotten much worse. Everyone says our vote matters, but until we can check the system and start taking a lot of that money out, I feel like it's just power . . . people with money have the power.
>
> —SCOTT HASSON, DENVER[5]

What I do know is that you can't really trust
anyone. It's all screwed up no matter who's
in the White House.

—SHARI PIZARRO, ST. PETERSBURG, FLORIDA[6]

Whether because of withdrawal or outrage, the voter turnout in the 2014 midterm election was abysmally low. About a
third of eligible voters went to the polls. According to the United
States Elections Project, the last time turnout was that low was
in the middle of World War II.[7] At least in 1942 the cause for
low turnout was that many voters were on the battlefield or
otherwise engaged in the war effort. What stopped two out of
three voters in 2014 was not fighting an external threat, like the
Nazis. It was the internal threat of disengagement from a political process that seemed fundamentally out of their control.

Divided State Legislatures

In theory, the capital of every state—from Sacramento to
Tallahassee, Austin to Lansing—is a "laboratory of democracy."
Unlike Capitol Hill, state legislatures are filled with neighbors
and people who know each other. Each is unique in the way
it plays the game of politics. But over the last few decades, as
hyperpolarization took hold, state legislatures have been more
dysfunctional than ever. While some states are more polarized
(California and Colorado) and others less polarized (Rhode
Island and Delaware), what is common across the nation is that
the partisan divide at the state level is growing. By some mea-
sures, more than half of all state legislatures are more polarized
than Congress.[8]

With state legislatures in charge of drawing the lines of
their own districts, this hyperpolarization is now built into the
system. As Republican State Senator Mark McDaniel of North

Carolina put it, "We [state legislators] are now in the business of rigging elections." Concurs Democratic Representative Jim Cooper of Tennessee: "Each party is working hard to create fewer competitive districts. . . . With a firm grip on their districts and no worries about alienating voters in the other party, gerrymandered extremists are often the loudest voices."[9]

Partisan Election Officials

"Imagine that the umpire in a baseball game was affiliated with one of the teams on the field," a CBS news reporter asked the viewing audience recently. "Would you trust him to call the game fairly?"[10]

Most Americans would immediately reply with a resounding "No!" Yet this is the way our system is structured. In most states (with a few notable exceptions), we have put partisan umpires in charge of the electoral game.

Most Americans do not even know that elections are administered by the states under the leadership of the secretary of state. In complete violation of what we have learned in sports, the person who is in charge of elections in each state is a member of one of the competing teams. "It is as if," says the American Enterprise Institute's Norm Ornstein, "one of the referees at the Super Bowl owned stock in one of the teams."[11]

The nation awakened to this fundamental problem in the cliffhanger election of 2000. The state of Florida determined whether George W. Bush or Al Gore would win the election for president of the United States of America. When the American people learned that the person in charge of administering the vote, Florida Secretary of State Katherine Harris, was a Republican who also happened to be Bush's state campaign chairperson, there was a momentary outcry. And then nothing changed.

The conflict of interest is so clear that even a child can understand it. How can the secretary of state act fairly if the "referee" is working for one of the competing teams? "It's an inherent conflict of interest because you've got an umpire who has a betting stake in the game," said Ohio State University law professor Daniel Tokaji, an expert in election law. "We can't know for sure whether Harris made the decisions she made because that was her legitimate interpretation of the law or she wanted to help Bush win," he said. "But this is not just a problem of bad actors; this is the problem of an inherently unfair system."[12]

Most Americans can probably name the commissioner of the National Football League. But how many of us can name the chairperson of the Federal Election Commission? The truth is: most citizens have never even heard of the FEC. That may be because the FEC does so little. It's been called "a joke" (by Tony Coelho, a Democrat) and "the little agency that can't" (by John McCain, a Republican). Independent watchdog agencies call it "designed for partisan stalemate."

The FEC is governed by six commissioners who by law are divided into "no more than three members from the same party." What this means, in practice, is that there are three Democrats and three Republicans. Four votes are required to take action. So even the most serious infractions of campaign finance law usually go unpunished—even when the FEC's own general counsel recommends that the commission take action.

Endless Campaigns

Today, campaigning never ends. That means governing never begins. What used to be called governing is now just positioning for the next election. Even if you are the president of the United States of America, you won't get much done if the government you run is suspended indefinitely in what one insider calls the "perma-campaign."[13] *You cannot serve the people if you never stop campaigning.*

In fact, "campaigns are not . . . campaigns," announced a front-page article in the *New York Times*. Referring to the emerging quests for the White House by Marco Rubio, Hillary Clinton, and Jeb Bush, the investigative report said that the word "campaign" was no longer an accurate way of describing the "intricate constellations of political committees, super PACs and tax exempt groups, engineered to avoid fundraising restrictions imposed on candidates and their parties after the Watergate scandal."[14]

That candidates claim to be serving us, the people, is no secret: they repeat this stock phrase like a mantra. While many candidates intend to do just that, they are caught in a set of rules that compels them to behave in ways that hurt others, hurt themselves, and hurt the country that they love.

Here are fragments of comments from some of the members of Congress with whom I have worked:

> "It is incredibly painful . . . and it just doesn't end with the campaign!"

> "If I had known it would be like this . . ."

> "Personally, I could handle it; it came with the territory. But I just didn't know how to protect my wife and kids."

> "I've served six terms, and I can't remember it ever being this poisonous."

> "It wasn't just my opponent. It was all these special-interest groups and their ads that made it so ugly."

"What's the point of working here if we can't even
conduct the people's business anymore?"

One consequence of hyperpartisanship is that campaigns
no longer serve the people because they no longer serve their
original purpose. How can we, the people, pick the "best
leader" when very often the best leaders have decided not to
run in the first place? When political campaigns become so
dirty—and so expensive—that good people won't run, how do
campaigns differ from street fights between warring gangs?

The organization in charge of elections, the Federal
Election Commission, is highly unlikely to fix the problem.
"People think the FEC is dysfunctional," said the chairwoman
of the Commission, Anne M. Ravel. "It's worse than dysfunctional." And it is not working because it's designed that way.
The three board members appointed by the Republican Party,
and the three appointed by the Democratic Party, are in a per-
petual deadlock.[15]

Broken Government

The feeling that government is broken is not a liberal or conservative attitude. It is present across the political spectrum. Both
Republican and Democratic candidates for president refer to it,
major newspapers editorialize about it, and ordinary citizens
across the spectrum recognize it. The feeling that government
is out of citizens' control is now almost universal.

"A year still has 365 days," says Tamera Luzzatto, the former chief of staff for Senators Clinton and Rockefeller. "The
week still has 7 days, and the day still 24 hours. Time has not
changed. But the amount of money these folks have to raise has
gone through the roof!"[16]

Because one-quarter of 1 percent of the people give
more than two-thirds of the money to candidates, the incen-

tives are strong to spend time listening to these big-pocket elites. According to the Democratic Congressional Campaign Committee, candidates now spend four hours a day on "call time"—a neutral-sounding, whitewashed term for raising big money from rich donors. Even when good candidates run, they are forced to be hyperpartisan fund-raisers to make it through the primaries. Most of their time is not spent legislating, studying issues, speaking to voters, or relaxing with their family. It is spent raising money from the 0.25 percent—which explains why so many Americans feel that we are moving toward what one Nobel Prize-winning economist calls government "of the 1 percent, for the 1 percent, and by the 1 percent."[17]

Nothing illustrates the need for structural change more vividly than the Commission on Presidential Debates (CPD), which even its own leaders criticize. The two major parties elbowed out the League of Women Voters in 1988 and grabbed control of the debate process. Ever since then, it has fallen into disrepute. Critics from across the political landscape have expressed their outrage that the gatekeepers for the most important and prestigious political debates in our national life are none other than the two competing teams. The revered anchorman Walter Cronkite called the CPD an "unconscionable fraud." Said conservative Republican Newt Gingrich: "The very concept of an elite commission deciding for the American people who deserves to be heard is profoundly wrong." Echoed an outraged Arianna Huffington, a liberal Democrat: "Why not skip the polling and just hire armed guards to gun down any threat to the two-party domination of the debates?" Steve Forbes called it "a corrupt duopoly." And John Culver, a former senator and director of the Commission, said derisively: "Where did these people come from to be the final arbiters of free speech?"[18]

Their outrage underscores the fact that the integrity of the political system itself is now in question. Candidates on both sides of the fence now often refer to the system as "dysfunctional." Some of the candidates go even further, like New Jersey Governor Chris Christie, a Republican, who announced his candidacy for president in the 2016 election by declaring: "Both parties have failed our country." President Obama himself acknowledged that politicians "are more interested in scoring points than getting things done."[19] As Republican pollster Frank Luntz reported after the 2014 elections: "From the reddest rural towns to the biggest bluest big cities, the sentiment is the same. People say Washington is broken and on the decline, and that government no longer works for them—only for the rich and powerful."[20]

Virtually all political analysts agree: each election is becoming more toxic, more expensive, and more partisan than the previous one. Whether we prefer Candidate A or Candidate B, whether we identify with the donkey or the elephant (or neither), whether we lean left or right, our partisan preferences have become political ghettos. We are building walls between ourselves, walls that are turning us often into strangers and sometimes even into enemies.

If both parties have failed our country, just working to make sure that our side wins is not enough. We also have to make sure that our victory, or our loss, serves more than our party—that it ultimately serves to reunite our country. Yes, every election cycle brings us a new political hero. Yes, the news media will dwell on personalities and ask, "Can he (or she) save America?" But clearly no one person can ensure that America fulfills its destiny. We must all take responsibility for leadership. No knight on a white horse will save America, but we can.

THE OPPORTUNITY

From Running Against
to Working With

To understand the full range of changes needed in our political system takes real commitment. It's not a quick fix. Our political system is complex, and so is the overhaul it requires. Systemic changes that are needed include taking away partisan control of drawing congressional districts, enabling candidates who are not associated with the two major parties to be on the ballot, and ensuring that money does not undermine either free speech or free elections. If we want to bridge the partisan divide, these structural changes are vital.[21]

But the reuniting of America does not depend only on systems. It also depends on you, and me, and ordinary American citizens like Amanda Kathryn Roman who are willing to take the journey beyond partisanship.

No one has ever recruited more college Republicans than Roman. "I broke records in every category," she says proudly. Fund-raising, recruitment, voter registration, volunteers, and new chapters: in every area she was a superstar. With amazing dedication, first in college and then working directly in politics, she helped weave together the center-right coalition in America.

But before long, Roman discerned what she calls the "underbelly" of partisan politics. In both parties she saw a lack of accountability, transparency, and integrity. Increasingly her work caused her to feel an "absence of the whole." She felt a yearning to elevate the voices of citizens—*all* citizens.

It was then that Roman encountered the movement to reunite America. "As a transpartisan, I choose to welcome and respect everyone; all have a seat at the table," she observes. "I don't have to give up my deeply held values or my beliefs. I can sit down with anyone to seek solutions that benefit the whole community. To me, being transpartisan is a spirit, a way of being a citizen that appreciates the wisdom in diversity."

For Roman, this is not theory but daily practice. As senior director for the Citizens Campaign in New Jersey, she coordinates a statewide community of problem solvers that includes government law and policy experts, citizen journalists, civic leaders, students, teachers, entrepreneurs—in fact, a cross-section of the state's citizens. The Campaign's network of citizen activists defines solutions this way: 1. cost-effective, 2. evidence based, 3. beneficial to the whole community, and 4. implemented with a no-blame approach.

Roman stresses the final ingredient because it is the opposite of partisan-driven politics. The Citizens Campaign refuses to be manipulated by either party and is committed to always working across the spectrum. Because of grassroots efforts like hers, the pressure is increasing for transforming campaign tactics into good governance.

In fact, in every one of the five areas where hyperpartisan media and politics have undermined our democracy, those who are reuniting America are working to repair and renew it. Recall, once again, that the new narrative of Story #3 is about "searching for common ground that can strengthen the country that we all love." Each of the following strands of the movement is playing a pivotal role in making that story come true:

Dynamic citizen engagement

Collaborative state legislatures

Trustworthy elections

Inspiring campaigns

Effective governance

Dynamic Citizen Engagement

Bridging the partisan divide does not begin in Washington. It begins in our hearts and minds. We can transform politics if we come together across our differences and then take the work to scale by applying new technologies and civic tools that fellow Americans like Carolyn Lukensmeyer have developed over the past generation.

During nearly twenty years as president of AmericaSpeaks, Lukensmeyer built an innovative citizen engagement methodology for bringing large numbers of people into complex and urgent decision-making processes—from helping to shape New Orleans's recovery plan after Hurricane Katrina to creating a new vision for Ground Zero following the September 11 attacks. Lukensmeyer's brilliant framework—laid out in detail in her book *Bringing Citizen Voices to the Table*—shows how citizen engagement can be the key to a healthy democracy. As Lukensmeyer notes, if only the extremes participate in our democracy, the ensuing hyperpartisanship ensures that no progress can be made on the significant issues facing our country. As more and more of the diversity that makes up America participates, the healthier our democracy will be.

Lukensmeyer's strategy for dynamic (as opposed to superficial) citizen engagement is based on seven interlocking principles:

- A link to decision makers

- Participant diversity

- Informed participation

- Facilitated deliberation

- Fast feedback

- Shared priorities and clear recommendations for action.

- Sustained citizen involvement

Evaluation studies show that these principles are effective. When they are applied, citizens put their differences aside to solve problems and find common ground—even on the most highly polarizing issues.

In 2010, for example, AmericaSpeaks took on the hot-button issue of addressing our national debt and deficit. Across nineteen sites, thirty-five hundred people—including members of local Tea Party groups and activists from MoveOn.org—came together to deliberate and develop shared views. Not only did participants find substantive agreement, but also they reported having learned from the experience and having been positively influenced by others' views and opinions. Before participating in the discussion, 90 percent of participants said they were very or somewhat dissatisfied with the tone and quality of political discussions. Afterward, 90 percent of the same group said they were very or somewhat satisfied with the discussions they had just experienced. So it is clear that with a safe environment, factual information, and an excellent design, voter cynicism and hyperpartisan hostility can be transformed into productive discourse.[22]

To build on this work, in 2012 Lukensmeyer became executive director of the National Institute for Civil Discourse. NICD was established in May 2011 after a gunman in Tucson killed six people and wounded thirteen—including former US Representative Gabrielle Giffords—who were participating in a "Congress on your Corner" event. NICD is, Lukensmeyer says, a "clarion call to all Americans to stand up and make their voices heard about the incivility and political dysfunction in our country today." With Presidents George Bush and Bill Clinton as honorary chairs, and former Senate Majority Leader Tom Daschle and US Supreme Court Justice Sandra Day O'Connor as honorary cochairs, NICD seeks to mobilize public will in order to create political will. NICD is skillfully working to build public demand for civil discourse and a government that works in the best interests of the country as a whole.

Collaborative State Legislatures

One of the most powerful efforts to increase collaborative problem solving at the state-government level is being undertaken by NICD through its Next Generation program. Created and led by former Democratic Representative Ted Celeste of Ohio, Next Generation works to cultivate a culture in which discourse and collaboration typify public policy development. "The reason we called our program Next Generation," Celeste told me, "is that the ultimate goal is a generation of state legislators who believe in creating common ground, and who will help their colleagues work toward this goal after they have moved on to the national level. Since 220 legislators in nine states have already experienced the Next Generation training process, we are rapidly forming a national network of state legislators committed to civil governance."

Celeste was inspired to create Next Generation by his personal experience of the dysfunction of hyperpartisan politics. He ran his first political campaign with an all-positive, cross-partisan message and, despite the odds, won and went on to serve three terms in the Ohio Legislature. But as he moved up the political ladder, he became increasingly troubled by the hyperpartisan toxicity he experienced and wanted to change the way the game was played. Next Generation's signature workshop—"Building Trust through Civil Discourse"—highlights the essential ingredients that Celeste and his colleagues believe will help legislators shift from partisan campaigning to consensus governing.

"Our mission is to work in as many states as possible, where legislators themselves invite us in," says Celeste. "We are creating a shared experience that leads legislators to change their behavior in ways that strengthen their capacity to govern. Part of the cross-party team-building process is generating their own ground rules. So we don't tell them what their ground rules are going to be; *they* tell *us*."

The part of the program that has the strongest impact on participants, Celeste believes, is a process called "Political Journey," in which lawmakers share how their political identity was shaped, decade by decade, through their personal experiences. Legislators record and share their personal stories, and the stories are posted on a wall so that all can see the group's collective political biography—both the similarities and the differences. This work sets the stage for taking on dysfunctional interactions and hyperpartisan habits.

Next Generation has made rapid and remarkable progress with legislators across the country. More cross-party breakthroughs are happening at the state level than most Americans could imagine. With fifty "laboratories of democracy," in the coming years we can expect to see a wide range of cross-partisan experiences from state capitals that will give national leaders new models for putting people before party.

Trustworthy Elections

To reunite America, an obvious starting point is the official who manages elections: the secretary of state. One model for reforming the electoral process that has proved highly effective is Wisconsin's Government Accountability Board. Created four years ago by the Wisconsin Legislature, the six-member Government Accountability Board is staffed with judges who have been out of partisan politics for at least half a dozen years and who collectively serve as an elections and ethics board. Despite the fact that it has threatened some politicians, it remains a model worth emulating. State leaders "should be bragging about and taking credit for the structure and accomplishments of the G.A.B.," said the board's director and general counsel proudly.[23]

If Wisconsin and other states can create a cross-spectrum management structure for elections, the obvious question is: why can't the United States of America do so?

The answer is: we can.

The principles of the Government Accountability Board could easily be applied to the Federal Election Commission. There is no reason why the FEC should be owned and operated by the two parties. Nowhere in the Constitution does it state that parties should control this vital institution. On the contrary, our country is a democratic republic, which means it is (1) a citizen-run government with (2) elected representatives. The Tenth Amendment of the Bill of Rights defines this with crystal clarity:

> The powers not delegated to the United States by the Constitution, nor prohibited by it to the States, are reserved to the States respectively, or to the people.

The powers not delegated to Washington are reserved for the states and the people. *There is no mention of parties at all.*

We could certainly find six or more distinguished transpartisan citizens to serve regular two-to-four year terms on a national Government Accountability Board. Instead of the six party appointees (half Democrats, half Republicans) who have watched the FEC that they "govern" be reduced to a laughingstock, the Board members would be independent of party interference and able to monitor elections and make decisions impartially.

But we cannot expect to create independent election watchdogs like the Government Accountability Board without encountering party opposition. Originally founded in 2007 with almost unanimous, bipartisan legislative support, the Board has already triggered opposition. Politicians whose campaigns the Board investigated have tried to limit its power. Even the Wisconsin Legislature has been threatened by it to the point that the speaker and the majority leader have tried to add partisan appointments to the purposefully nonpartisan board![24]

Not surprisingly, party leaders are trying to maintain party control. "Since election law is created by state legislatures," Linda Killian reminds us, "it is written to benefit the two parties, who operate a virtually closed system in which they make all the rules. Independents have no representation on any of the bodies that regulate elections, from the Federal Election Commission to state and local boards of elections."

When we are more confident that the first loyalty of officials managing elections will be to their state, not their party, we will also be more likely to have confidence in the electoral process itself. That confidence requires that the ballot be open to qualified citizens regardless of whether they are members of the two-party club.

While no single organization represents all Independent voters, scores of initiatives share the same objective: amplifying the voice of the invisible non-party-member majority in America. Open primaries mean that all voters, even those who are not registered with a party, can vote in a primary—and the top two vote-winners enter a runoff. Many advocates of these reforms are part of EndPartisanship.org, a remarkable coalition of organizations dedicated to the principle that all voters—even those not affiliated with a political party—have equal rights in the election process. More than five hundred Independents and other networks representing nonaffiliated voters, for example, gathered in March 2015 in New York City under the auspices of IndependentVoting.org. Others use the term *centrist* to describe themselves and get involved in organizations like the Centrist Project or Third Way.

"I am a member of the *anti*-party!" shouted Jackie Salit, the outspoken leader of IndependentVoting.org, galvanizing her audience. Working together, she predicted, the "independent movement" would reach its fundamental goal of opening up primaries so that they would have a voice in elections just like card-carrying Democrats and Republicans.

During every election cycle, Salit pressures candidates of both parties to make room for Independents. In 2015, she focused on a state with a very high percentage of Independents: Arizona. In a gutsy editorial in the *Arizona Republic* titled "Are voting rights for all voters? Let's ask Hillary!" she directly challenged the candidates to address "the rights of Independent voters and the need to reform the primary system to make it inclusive." Reacting to Hillary Clinton's statement that our political system was "so paralyzed in gridlock," Salit challenged all the candidates to "give all voters—including Independents—the chance to vote and to build bridges together, regardless of party affiliation."

> If you are not prepared to challenge your own party to fight for voter freedom for all the American people, then you shouldn't be president. And that goes for [all] the rest. When they come to Arizona, the independents will have to tell them so.[25]

Not only outsiders like Jackie Salit but also insiders such as former Mayor Paul Johnson of Phoenix are echoing this call for opening up elections. "People are being silenced by the architecture of the system," says Johnson bluntly. When Johnson describes the details in his home state of Arizona—specifically that it costs far more and requires far more signatures to get on the ballot as an Independent than as a "D" or an "R"—it is hard to argue with his conclusion: "The system is rigged to keep people out."[26]

Even inside-the-Beltway politicians in the US House and Senate are joining the chorus of voices challenging our increasingly dysfunctional duopoly. "We can't let 535 people continue to limit the progress of a nation of more than three hundred million," said Representative John K. Delaney (D-Maryland). Backed by his colleague Tom Cole (R-Oklahoma), the two congressmen are promoting the Open Our Democracy Act, which is designed to give Independents and non-party members a voice in primary elections. Their goal: "to make the House of Representatives actually representative."[27]

According to Senator Charles Schumer (D-New York) and several other elected officials of both parties, American politics may appear healthy on the outside because of the numerical balance of Democrats and Republicans, but closed primaries have a profoundly distorting impact. "Closed primaries," says Schumer, "poison the health of that system and warp its natural balance." Those who come out to vote in closed primaries are "the 10 percent at each of the two extremes of the political spectrum. Making things worse, in most states, laws prohibit Independents—who are not registered with either party and who make up a growing proportion of the electorate—from voting in primaries at all. . . . For those of us who are in despair over partisanship and polarization in Congress, reform of the primary system is a start."[28]

This reform is not rocket science. More than a dozen states are already experimenting with various forms of open primaries. If our generation is to build a bridge across the partisan divide in America, this is a fundamental part of its foundation.

Inspiring Campaigns

"Multiplicity in choice is what the millennials have grown up with," argues Jon Avlon, editor in chief of the online news source the *Daily Beast*, highly favored by this generation. "They don't have to buy the album, just have to buy the song. That's what they are used to. To conclude that these young people self-declaring as independents simply don't know what they believe—that they're just uninformed people who don't know what they want—seems awfully condescending to me. It's totally missing the mark."

Unwilling to recognize this (r)evolution-in-progress, cynics claim that the skyrocketing number of millennial Independents don't really exist because they all lean left or right, and so their self-identification can be ignored. But as old mainstream media obsess about the Democrats and Republicans, the new media are giving the rising generations a much wider range of choices.

Run for America is running younger, nontraditional, entrepreneurial-oriented candidates who will go directly to the people. "We are political entrepreneurs," says twenty-seven-year-old Run for America founder David Burstein. "The current qualification [for candidates] is how many political connections do you have and how much money can you raise. That tends to lead—surprise, surprise—to people who are exactly like the current politics and are thus part of the problem."

Burstein has no patience for people who dismiss politics as too broken or too dysfunctional. That attitude, he maintains, simply gives "more and more control to the same forces and the same people who have made it as broken as it is." Instead, Run for America is promoting candidates who "have proven track records as outside-of-the-box thinkers as people who defy the status quo."[29]

Will Run for America's slate of candidates crack the campaign code and get elected? Although it's too soon to tell, the spirit of the new generation is already being felt. Tired of partisan stalemate, turned on by technological innovation, the emerging generations are an instinctively boundary-crossing political and cultural force. Poisonous partisanship has been going on for so long that the younger generations have seen nothing but political dysfunction. For this reason, they tend to see why being hyperpartisan is a dead end more quickly than many of their elders. They are less enamored of political parties, and partisanship, than any generation before. Across the board—culturally as well as politically—their generation is saying a powerful "no" to stereotypical boxes.[30]

Like the millennials, more and more candidates are ready to try something new. Precisely because so many voters are fed up with polarization, running a campaign that connects rather than divides is becoming a more attractive, if still unorthodox, option. It takes very little imagination or courage to stand up in front of your own party faithful and tell them that you are one of them. A new and more daring course for a campaign is to hold events that cross boundaries and prove that the candidate can listen to and respect *everyone* across the political spectrum.

All such courageous candidates have to do is invite an audience that reflects America: roughly one-third Democrat, one-third Republican, and one-third Independent. With the heat-seeking media paying rapt attention, everyone would wonder how candidates would handle the competing views among the audience. They would be able to listen as voters gave voice openly and vulnerably to sharply contrasting views. It would be their golden opportunity to show that they could listen to *all* their constituents and then demonstrate that their position grew out of their capacity to lead the *whole* community.

Candidates do not need to throw out their own partisan, bring-out-the-base strategy. But they do need to reach out beyond their comfort zone and host some town meetings that break the mold. If they can show that they are running for office by building community, not dividing it, they will pick up votes from those who admire their courage and recognize that their campaign serves something greater than themselves.

This campaign-for-the-whole approach is sound regardless of whether a candidate is behind in the polls, way ahead, or in a tight race. If they are way behind, they need something to jolt their campaign and get attention. If they are way ahead, they can afford to take the risk. And if they are in a close race, then every undecided vote counts. In all three cases, they distinguish themselves by showing independent-minded, undecided voters that they can connect with the vast majority of their constituents, not just their narrow ideological tribe.

Obviously, this kind of campaign will be much more practical if the shift from closed to open primaries accelerates across the country. When open primaries spread to a state, the pressure to reach across the partisan divide in order to win will only grow.

Effective Governance

Once upon a time "there were two distinct seasons—a campaigning one and a governing one," recalls Norm Ornstein.
"Campaign consultants and pollsters used to disappear after
elections, but now they stick around as consultants, aides, lobbyists, ever present."[31]

Mickey Edwards, who served as a Republican congressman from Oklahoma in that era, experienced this shift. When
he first took the oath of office, he imagined that he "had crossed
an invisible line from candidate and partisan to legislator. This
line is no longer crossed."[32]

Since then, no one in America has done more than Edwards
to help ensure that this line between campaigning and governing is redrawn. After leaving government service, he taught at
Harvard University's Kennedy School of Government, where
he noticed the low regard that many of his students had for
politics. "To many young people observing politics," Edwards
wrote, "the narrowness and nastiness and partisan warfare they
see far outweighs the advantages and allure. Just as political
parties now find it hard to recruit good potential candidates, I
found it truly difficult to persuade my students to jump into the
political arena."[33]

So when Aspen Institute President Walter Isaacson invited him to help launch the Rodel Fellowship program for
government officials, which would give them the opportunity
to meet across political lines and learn together how to govern
better, he said yes. "It is time to work for change—to do what
we can to refocus American politics on achievement rather
than division, on big ideas and fundamental beliefs rather
than petty differences and slick campaign promises," Edwards
concluded. "And if we do it right, maybe before long, promis-

ing young students like mine might not flinch at the idea of a career in politics, but embrace it as full of hope, honor, and potential."[34]

After a decade under Edwards's leadership, current and past fellows include cabinet members, governors, mayors, members of Congress, and a legion of state legislators. With powerful cross-boundary experience under their belts, they are bringing a new spirit of collaboration and problem solving to governance in America. As a result, citizens who were previously uninspired by politics are getting engaged.

David Nevins, now a major supporter of the Rodel Fellowship, was so inspired by it that he launched his own leadership program at his alma mater, Penn State University. But until his sixties, he was a businessman who never had anything to do with politics. Although he followed the news and was well informed, he found politics "baffling."

"I couldn't believe how dysfunctional governance and politics are," he says, matter-of-factly.

Then one day he happened to see an interview with one of the founders of No Labels. Their bridge-building, problem-solving approach appealed to his practical business sensibility, and his commitment deepened.

"I learned there were thousands of citizens throughout the country," Nevins recalls, "who were just as frustrated as I was with the lack of civility . . . the crippling partisanship . . . the gridlock. I became a supporter of the Aspen Institute's Rodel Fellowship, and then, I started a democracy leadership program at my alma mater, Penn State University. And now I am both working for, and helping to create from scratch, the Bridge Alliance so that all these amazing organizations can start to work together!"

But as powerful as individual transformation may be, the system must be transformed as well. The only way to change the game is to change the rules. Congress must find practical ways, in committee and in the legislative process on the floor, for across-the-aisle partnerships to function more effectively. Instead of only partisan one-upmanship being incentivized, genuine problem solving by cross-party pairs and teams must become an integral part of congressional culture. As Jason Grumet, executive director of the Bipartisan Policy Center, aptly says, to reunite America, we need "two hands on the wheel."[35]

This urgent, practical goal is within sight. But the next stage of the journey depends on more than any one organization alone. The two questions we must now answer are: Can many powerful organizations and visionary leaders from across the political spectrum join together so that we, the people, can find a new path? Can we look beyond the forced choice of turning left or turning right, and move forward together toward a united future?

PART II

A MOVEMENT
BEING BORN

Democracy needs a place to sit down.

—HANNAH ARENDT

AS EVIDENCED BY the remarkable and eloquent citizens we met in part 1, the elements of a movement to reunite America are already present and are touching millions of lives. Whether you are a millennial who wants your generation to get a fair chance, a parent looking out for your children's welfare, a citizen wanting a more productive state legislature or Congress, or someone concerned about a specific issue such as criminal justice reform, there is an organization to which you can turn.

Without a doubt, the diverse organizations profiled in the preceding chapters are valiantly doing their part to bridge the partisan divide. But, taken together, do they represent a coherent alternative to hyperpartisan politics? Is Story #3—Americans working together with people different from ourselves to find common ground that can strengthen the country we all love— only a story? Or can it become a movement that truly reunites America?

In part 2, we explore the answers to these questions. We will look at the dramatic rise of Independents, explore the scope and name of this new movement, and reflect on precisely why it is emerging now. Finally, we will show why the old left–right political spectrum no longer charts the way forward but traps us in a hyperpartisan labyrinth from which there is no exit. Instead, when we begin to draw the outlines of a new map of the political terrain, the path ahead opens up before us. It is the path that the Founding Fathers began more than two centuries ago and that we must now rediscover anew.

FIVE

BORN OUT OF CRISIS

*Exploring the Movement
to Reunite America*

Having banished from our land that religious
intolerance under which mankind so long bled and
suffered, we have yet gained little if we countenance
a political intolerance as despotic [and] as wicked.

—PRESIDENT THOMAS JEFFERSON,
INAUGURAL ADDRESS, 1801[1]

IF WE DESTROY our civic environment, we become, as
President Abraham Lincoln warned, "a house divided." The
Bible is clear about what happens next: "Every city or house
divided against itself cannot stand."[2]

In response to this internal threat, American citizens, as
we have seen in part 1, are taking action. The men and women
profiled in the preceding pages are a combination of conservative and liberal, traditional and progressive, libertarian and independent. They don't fit in boxes. They look at each issue on
its merits. They refuse to be categorized by a label or defined by
a poll. They are free, independent American citizens—and there
are millions of them. Yet, if you read the news these days, you
wouldn't even know that this independence movement existed.

Independents are the largest and fastest-growing voting
bloc in the country. Gallup observes: "The 46% independent
identification in the fourth quarter of 2013 is a full three percentage points higher than Gallup has measured in any quarter during its telephone polling era."[3] In addition, almost out
of sight are the 40 percent of the American people who didn't
bother to vote in the last presidential election. Four out of ten of
our fellow citizens have already disassociated themselves from
the two brightly colored characters that are dominating the action at the front of the stage.

Most hyperpartisans do not want to face the fact that the
numbers of Independents and nonvoters have reached record

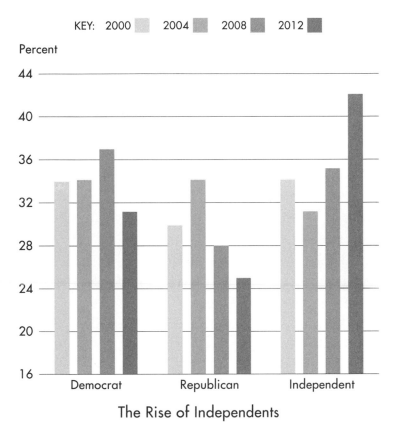

KEY: 2000 ▨ 2004 ▨ 2008 ▨ 2012 ■

The Rise of Independents

highs.[4] But the trend is crystal clear. During the last three years, the number of Independent voters has risen to more than 40 percent—and, as Gallup observes, "these are also the only years in Gallup's records that the percentage of independents has reached that level."

If more than four out of ten of us voters—and more than five out of ten young voters[5]—are Independent, why are almost none of our political leaders? Why is all the news coverage always about the two lowest bars in the graph shown here and never about the highest one? Why is there no headline news that, in the year 2013 alone, the number of Independents skyrocketed?

Like a magician doing card tricks, the pundits and experts on both left and right make the Independents disappear with sleight of hand. According to the prevailing narrative, the United States of America is divided into two camps that are increasingly at war with each other. But the facts show that this is simply not true. A larger fraction of citizens identify themselves as *neither* red nor blue than are members of the Democratic or Republican parties. They are not part of that simplistic two-sided story that dominates the news. All of us are being shown a self-portrait of the nation that is profoundly incomplete.

Like the early environmental movement, the movement to reunite America is still largely invisible. Before Rachel Carson wrote *Silent Spring*, which was embraced by President John F. Kennedy and then translated into law by President Richard M. Nixon, there were biologists, toxicologists, oceanographers, atmospheric scientists, embryologists, and so on—but no visible, definable environmental movement. Today, no responsible parent, liberal or conservative, wants to turn the clock back to an era of unregulated dirty air, contaminated water, and carcinogenic chemicals in the soil, food, products, etc. While some of us may have legitimate reservations about the regulations of the Environmental Protection Agency, which the Nixon Administration established in 1970, most of us are nevertheless grateful that our children have a healthier, safer environment than would otherwise have been our legacy to them.

Today, diverse groups are forming a loosely knit, diverse movement because toxins are polluting the civic environment. Although they are managing cities, running organizations, and solving problems with stakeholders from across the political spectrum, this legion of Americans has not clearly shared an identity as a movement—until now. There are literally thousands of organizations and hundreds of thousands of individuals who are bridging the divide. Just as business, government, and ordinary citizens all have a role to play in cleaning up our air, water, and soil, all of these sectors need to be involved in building a healthy, vibrant, twenty-first-century civic culture.

In every election, pundits and pollsters contrast the leading Democrat and the leading Republican. Donors line up to support one army or the other. Generals compete to be in charge of the two armies. Cities compete for the right to host the two polarized multimillion-dollar conventions where the two combatting armies rally their troops, denounce their enemy, and boldly proclaim that they will win in November.

But does this narrative have to do with our future? Does it really capture who "we, the people" are? Or does it depict only a small part of the electorate—who are then reduced to "conservative" and "liberal" stereotypes? Meanwhile, where do the rest of us—the majority of Americans—gather to express ourselves and to be heard?

This movement to reunite America is emerging now because normal, healthy partisanship has morphed into a cancerous hyperpartisanship that feeds on itself. It is not about authentic, heartfelt differences of values and interests. It is about party-driven, hyped-up, knee-jerk opposition to everything the other side stands for. Not only are we divided about almost every public policy; we are divided now even in times of crisis. For a brief, shining moment following the terrorist attacks on September 11, 2001, it seemed that a new enemy might bring us together. But the unity was fleeting. We have managed to become even more divided.

After Hurricane Katrina devastated New Orleans in 2005, the story quickly shifted from homeless and broken neighborhoods to attacking President Bush's ineffective response.

Following the rapid collapse of banks and other financial institutions during the 2008 financial crisis, the slow and painful recovery was marred by charges and countercharges, with extremists in each party blaming the other for causing the economic calamity.

During their confrontation about the debt ceiling in 2013, President Obama and House Speaker John Boehner failed to reach agreement and blamed each other for the government shutdown.

With delicate nuclear negotiations between the United States and Iran underway in early 2015, the spectacle of American foreign policy in hyperpartisan disarray undermined our nation's authority and credibility. Instead of being unified by fighting a common enemy, presidential candidates during the 2016 election cycle accused each other over conduct of the wars in Afghanistan and Iraq while impugning the judgment of President Bush or President Obama.

When even crises and wars cannot unite us, it is an indicator that the toxicity of hyperpartisanship has reached new and dangerous levels. Any doubt about this was dispelled by one of the most thorough studies ever undertaken on the subject, *Political Polarization in the American Public: How Increasing Ideological Uniformity and Partisan Antipathy Affect Politics, Compromise and Everyday Life*.[6] It proves that decades of corrosive mistrust have taken their toll on the basic civic bonds that hold America together. Differences have escalated into disrespect: record numbers of Americans now consider the other party "threatening the nation's well-being."

Fortunately, a new generation of leaders is challenging us to love our country in a new way. To evolve from enemies to adversaries, from adversaries to rivals, and from rivals to partners—this is the catalytic role of the emerging movement to bridge the partisan divides.

WHAT WILL THE MOVEMENT BE CALLED?

Some of our colleagues who focus directly on organizing non-party members call it the *independence* movement. By contrast, others whose attention centers on the two major parties call it the *bipartisan* movement. Still others who are committed to the structural reforms we explored in chapter 4 call it the *democracy reform* movement. There are others who are so committed to increasing the voices of citizens that they call it the *civic engagement* movement. And finally, there are those who care deeply about how we communicate and refer to the *civility* movement.

A clue to another potential name for the movement is embedded in former Republican Congressman Mickey Edwards's seminal book *The Parties Versus the People*. One of the chapters is titled "Beyond Partisanship."[7] This phrase, or its one-word synonym *transpartisan*, captures the essence of Story #3.

> **Story #1:** Conservatives are right and, if elected, will strengthen America.
>
> **Story #2:** Liberals are right and, if elected, will strengthen America.
>
> **Story #3:** Americans can work *together* with people different from ourselves to find common ground that can strengthen the country that we all love.

From my perspective, transpartisans are responding to the threat of hyperpartisanship in three fundamental ways: *who* ("people different from ourselves"), *how* (finding "common ground"), and *why* ("to strengthen the country that we all love").

Calling the movement "transpartisan" because it is beyond partisanship does not mean, however, that we must suddenly wipe clean the slate of our identity. Of course we still have our points of view. As libertarian Michael Ostrolenk points out, being transpartisan does not require us to "abandon [our] partisan worldviews." Rather, it means a willingness "to recognize that people legitimately have different worldviews. . . . Transpartisanship is not about avoiding conflict, but about *transforming* conflict to promote new ways of thinking."[8]

Looking back to the beginning of our journey, that last phrase describes perfectly what the ten inspiring members of the Bipartisan Retreat Committee were doing. They were taking all of their perspectives—which ranged across the political spectrum—and standing together for something that transcended their partisan objectives. So Story #3 is fundamentally a *transpartisan* story. It is about returning to the essence of what keeps the United States united.

Perhaps because he has helped catalyze this field for several decades and knows its history, my colleague John Steiner sees tremendous value in the word *transpartisan*. He traces it as far back as the early 1980s, when Don Beck used the term to show how to integrate various mind-sets in such diverse cultures as those in South Africa, the Middle East, and the United States. (In 2000, I cowrote with Beck a transpartisan memo to then-presidential candidate George W. Bush in which we both promoted the concept.) Steiner also acknowledges the pathfinding American scholar Gene Sharp's use of the term in his work that helped catalyze the Arab Spring and civic empowerment movements throughout the world. More recently, the publication in 2008 of *Voice of the People: The Transpartisan Imperative in American Life,* by A. Lawrence Chickering and James S. Turner, was a turning point for the field. Similarly, the key movers behind the Bipartisan Policy Center, although still two-party oriented in their approach, are eloquent advocates of this more visionary approach.

While relatively unfamiliar, this new word is nevertheless widely used. It has almost forty thousand entries in a Google search and can be found everywhere from the liberal *Washington Post* to the conservative Cato Institute, from *The Daily Show* to the libertarian-led Liberty Coalition, from Accuracy.org to the Hewlett Foundation. But this neologism may still strike many citizens, as well as many members of the movement itself, as awkward.

"Trans*portation*?" said the middle-aged businesswoman who attended a "Transpartisan Leadership" lecture in Louisville, Kentucky. "At first, I thought you were inviting me to a meeting about mass transit. Then I thought maybe it was another word: trans*sexual.* But then I looked more closely, and I realized I didn't know *what* it meant."

"Don't use that word here," said a colleague in Kansas City. "People here won't understand it. And if they do, they won't like it."

"Trans-*what*?" asked a participant in a citizen dialogue in Fresno. "Folks won't have anything to do with that weird name."

"Whatever citizens may wish to call this dynamic," Steiner says, "I am grateful to all of the courageous bridge builders who are part of the emerging transpartisan movement. The way they are putting their love for our country before party into action is ushering in a new political era for America."

THE MOVEMENT'S ESSENCE:
VENTURING BEYOND PARTISANSHIP

The word, ultimately, is not what matters. It is the spirit that infuses it. Some of the strongest voices in the movement do not even use the word. In fact, an organization that is connecting many of the leaders profiled in part 1 chose *not* to call itself the Transpartisan Alliance but instead chose the name the Bridge Alliance. Whatever term we may prefer, let us focus on what we know to be true.

We all know how oneness, unity, and connection feel. Our communities, our schools, our transportation systems, our businesses, would not function without the millions of patriotic American citizens who are working across party lines together every day as neighbors and colleagues. In the broadest sense of the word, every successful marriage in which two partners find common ground is transpartisan. So is every parent who raises children with love and firmness. So is every community that deals with competing interests and every company that responsibly juggles the interests of all its stakeholders. The challenge is to apply what we already know in these spheres of life to the contentious, high-stakes, and often far more treacherous terrain of politics.

Whether we are Democrats or Republicans, Independents or libertarians, or some other distinct self-definition (such as the ever-popular "fiscal conservative, social liberal"), it is this connective energy—of what President Lincoln called "fraternal feelings"—that holds together the United States of America. It is the motor oil that keeps the engine of the American economy running. While ultimately it may require a name, what is more important now is to recognize the spirit—a new, fresh, more inclusive way of loving our country that can renew and revitalize our public life.

As we clearly showed in part 1, the movement is emerging because of both the hyperpartisan *danger* and the historic transpartisan *opportunity*. During precisely the same period when American politics became increasingly divided, American culture was developing unprecedented methods for connecting and working together. While social media can be abused, they can also be harnessed. Thanks to high-tech breakthroughs and pioneering civic initiatives, our capacity as a nation to converse with one another and resolve problems has never been greater.

On the high-tech frontier, Microsoft, Apple, Google, Twitter, and other Silicon Valley companies are providing dazzling tools for communicating that would have absolutely astounded the Founding Fathers. With cellphones in hand, citizens can register their opinions instantly in large numbers. With audio and video computer links, networks of citizens can debate and dialogue across time and distance. If we invested in this infrastructure and applied it to civic engagement, we could literally have a national conversation engaging every citizen who wished to participate. All that is needed is for these pioneering companies to be as imaginative as citizens as they are as technicians.

This historic movement, still young, was indeed born out of crisis. But it will grow and mature because the American spirit of ingenuity, adventure, and hard work will turn this civic crisis into an exciting opportunity for a high-tech, high-touch national conversation that can renew our political culture.

But to reunite America amid intensifying, genuine conflict is a long, challenging journey. To find our way forward, we need a better map.

SIX

MAPPING
THE FUTURE

*Transforming Conflict
into Opportunity*

> The greatest threat in times of turbulence is not the
> turbulence; it is to act with yesterday's logic.
>
> —Peter Drucker[1]

TO REUNITE AMERICA, our challenge is to integrate and unify the best of both left and right. We must take the intelligence of conservatism and liberalism and apply it wisely and pragmatically to the challenges that our country faces. But to do so, we have to free ourselves from the obsolete political map that maintains that doing so is impossible. In this high-tech era, we need to update our civic software.

We already know the direction we want to go. In various ways, all of our leaders, no matter where they fall on the political spectrum, have pointed to the same mountaintop. They all say that our goal is ultimately not to veer left or right but to go forward. Just listen to what they have said to us on their way to the White House:

> For some time now we've all fallen into a pattern of describing our choice as Left or Right. But is that really an accurate description of the choice before us? Isn't our choice really not one of Left or Right, but of up or down? (Ronald Reagan)[2]

> Before we are Republicans or Democrats, liberals or conservatives, or any of the other labels that divide us, we are Americans, all with a personal stake in our country. (Bill Clinton)[3]

> I'm a uniter, not a divider . . . I know how to unite people. I don't like the politics of pitting one group of people against another, the politics of pointing fingers. I like the politics advocated by somebody like Ronald Reagan, who was a uniter. He didn't stand up and pit groups of people against each other. (George W. Bush)[4]

We remain more than a collection of red states and blue states. We are, and forever will be, the United States of America. (Barack Obama)[5]

These four presidents, like most of us, know that putting country before party and finding unity out of diversity is our challenge.

TOWARD A NEW POLITICAL MAP: UPDATING OUR CIVIC SOFTWARE

Like the early explorers of this continent, however, our leaders are using a flawed, outdated, incomplete, and misleading map. If we were taking a trip, none of us would rely on a map that was more than two hundred years old. If we have a smartphone, we prefer to get the latest updates. Yet today we are still using a political map that dates back to the French Revolution. When the Legislative Assembly met in Paris in 1789, those who still supported the monarch and its loyal aristocracy sat on the right. Those who opposed it sat on the left. And so was born the political map that we still use today.

The Left–Right Line

FAR LEFT ——— LEFT ——— CENTER ——— RIGHT ——— FAR RIGHT
(Liberal)   (Moderate)   (Conservative)

When you look at this line, does it make sense to you? Do you fit easily on this line? When you try to do so, do you feel it reflects the richness and depth of what you personally believe?

My colleagues and I asked these questions several years ago at a meeting of leaders of American mass-membership organizations from across the political spectrum. They ranged from left-of-center organizations like MoveOn.org and Common Cause to right-of-center organizations like the Christian Coalition and Americans for Tax Reform, as well as moderate or nonpartisan organizations like AARP. Collectively they had a membership of tens of millions of Americans. We showed the participants the above map of the political spectrum and asked them: "Does this map accurately describe your experience of the political landscape today?"

Unanimously, they said *no*. Literally every participant in the meeting agreed that the old map was misleading, one-dimensional, and inherently divisive. Every one of them believed that we Americans inhabit a landscape far more complex and filled with possibilities. Since four out of five Americans do not consider themselves either "consistent liberals" or "consistent conservatives," we need a better map that includes this independent-minded, non-party-member majority.[6]

Unfortunately, without a new map, we continue to use the old one—and continue to get lost. More than a century after the political philosopher John Stuart Mill defined conservatism and liberalism, the ends of the political spectrum still try to follow Mill's obsolete definitions of the right (the "party of order and stability") and the left (the "party of progress and reform").[7] The old map still mesmerizes many of us so completely that we cannot see beyond it or even begin to imagine an alternative. But when we look at it with a fresh eye, it begins to lose its power to hypnotize us.

Even today, when well-meaning people try to define the difference between the parties of the left and the right, the definitions sound like an idiot's multiple-choice quiz. The well-intentioned author of the nonpartisan political primer *What You Should Know About Politics . . . but Don't*, endorsed by former presidential candidates Walter Mondale (Democrat) and Bob Dole (Republican), wrote her book to simplify politics for the average voter. It is painful to witness her valiant struggle to define the two major parties:

> Republicans believe that the free market should be left alone and that government should get out of the way. Democrats believe that the market can be unfair and that government is needed to help people and make the system work better.

Because this definition is neither exciting nor illuminating, the author tries again:

> Democrats want to regulate economic life and stay out of individuals' personal lives, while Republicans want as little economic regulation as possible but often support laws regulating moral behavior.[8]

The problem with defining the Democratic and Republican parties is not the author's. The problem is that when one splits the truth in half, one is left with two half-truths.

The question is not whether government should be involved in the economy, but how. The question is not whether there should be laws regulating moral behavior, but what those laws should, and should not, be. If we need half-truths and polarized clichés in order to join this two-party drama that today is turning quickly from farce to tragedy, we need a better choice than these two dead-ends.

With genuine respect for these two dueling political philosophies, let's remember that conservatism and liberalism were not divinely ordained. God may have created heaven and earth, and separated light from darkness. But God did not create left and right—we did. And it is now time to free ourselves from this paralyzing straitjacket.

To reunite America, we need a new map of the political landscape.

"The old political map was primarily created by a set of privileged male political philosophers living in an era of empire, the subjugation of women, colonization and slavery," Betsy Hall McKinney, the founder of the cross-spectrum women's initiative It's Time Network, reminds us. "They were all male political philosophers from a previous era. Karl Marx, Adam Smith—all of them were caught in the male-dominant abstractions and generalizations. Without the perspective of feminine experience and equally empowered relationships, the map is inherently incomplete."[9]

Like many others working to bridge the many divides that split our country today, McKinney recognizes that we have no idea what a new map would look like if *all of us*, women and men from a rich diversity of backgrounds, created it anew. "The new map has yet to be drawn," she acknowledges, "but it would certainly include respecting differences, and recognizing both our independence and our *inter*dependence. When it comes to those values, and promoting partnership and cooperation, women obviously have much to contribute."[10]

Why, McKinney and her colleagues ask, should *women* be divided against each other by a political map drawn by *men?*

Instead of letting male-dominated party structures define their issues, women's networks on the right and the left are engaged in their own woman-to-woman, often heated dialogues. Of course women differ as widely as men. The groups include progressive networks (like the National Organization for Women), centrist initiatives (like the League of Women Voters, It's Time 2015, and MomsRising.org), and conservative women's organizations (ranging from Concerned Women for America and the Eagle Forum to a new generation of "right of center" organizations like the Independent Women's Forum, the Clare Boothe Luce Policy Institute, the Network of Enlightened Women, Smart Girl Politics, and the Susan B. Anthony List). However, there is a growing chorus of women's voices uniting around a determination to find their own areas of agreement—and disagreement. Perhaps this is why the bridge builders in times of crisis—for example, Republican Senator Susan Collins during the 2013 government shutdown and Democratic Senator Patty Murray during the 2015 budget crisis—are often women.[11]

But it is not only women who want a different map. So do many others who cannot accept the one-dimensional left-right map. Many business leaders, for example, refuse to define themselves by this political dichotomy. Thoughtful entrepreneurs and economists do not agree that producing goods and services, the heart of economic activity, is fundamentally about a choice between left and right. When managed effectively with sound principles, argues economist Rajendra Sisodia, business is "not a question of left or right but a question of rising higher." If one examines the strongest, most socially responsible businesses, he says, the left–right "divides start to go away and actually start to look a bit silly."[12]

Of course real, substantive political and economic differences do exist. But to identify the *real* differences, and work them through to effective resolutions, cannot happen until we update our civic software and draw a better map.

What if we had an upgrade to Political Map 1.0? What if Map 2.0 reflected independent-minded American citizens as well as hard-core party members? What if it gave us the freedom to be liberal about some issues and conservative about

others? What if it distinguished between those who were willing to work with and learn from others across the spectrum—
and those who weren't?

A new generation of diverse political philosophers will
one day draw Map 2.0. Their twenty-first-century map, going
far beyond the one-dimensional left–right line, might include
a horizontal line contrasting various strands of liberalism and
conservatism (the *what*) and a vertical line contrasting *unum*
and *pluribus* (the *how*).

Whether the new map ultimately resembles this version or
not, it will certainly give us a second and vital dimension that
goes beyond the old partisan divide. It will reflect that we, the
people, have both heads *and* hearts. We can differ on *what* we
believe, and we can differ on *how* we want to resolve those differences. We can choose what kind of conservative or liberal we
want to be, and on which issues; *and* we can choose whether
and when to refuse to compromise and stick to our partisan positions. As citizens in the Public Square, we are not predestined
to polarize; we are empowered to work together when it serves
our country. By making more room for the many (*pluribus*), the
Public Square actually keeps us one (*unum*).

If we want to honor the true diversity of America, then
let's honor our unity as well. It is through a unified renewal of
our democracy that all the silent voices can one day finally be
heard. For true unity is not about conformity; on the contrary,
it is about the rich tapestry of Story #3: working together across
our differences to find common ground that can strengthen the
country that we all love.

This foursquare diagram also makes it clear that conservatives can and will disagree with their fellow conservatives, just
as liberals will disagree with others on the left. It reflects the
reality that these categories are neither monolithic nor frozen,

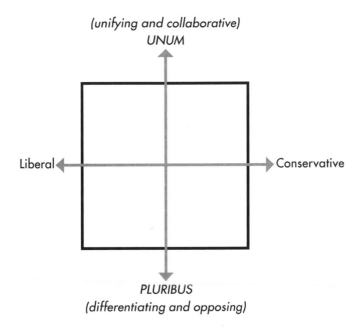

(unifying and collaborative)
UNUM

Liberal ←——————————————————→ Conservative

PLURIBUS
(differentiating and opposing)

The Public Square

but often hide as much as they reveal. Most important, this map enhances our capacity to think for ourselves and to work with others different from ourselves if and when we feel that best serves the country we love.

The primary way in which conservatives and liberals differ, according to scholars in the transpartisan field such as Chickering and Turner, is along the lines of freedom and order.[13] This diagram of the Public Square (as opposed to the left–right line) is meant to signify a *range* of liberal and conservative positions, not just one. On the left–right line, the extreme ends defined the terrain. But in the Public Square, we each can consult our own direct experience rather than feeling forced to recite a party platform. When we consult our own personal knowledge, even our bodies tell us that left and right are part of a whole.

BRIDGING POLARITIES:
THE CHALLENGE OF SEEING
THE WHOLE

"Who would choose to live their life with only a left or right hand?" asks William Ury, coauthor of *Getting to Yes* and a close colleague with whom I have often cofacilitated transpartisan dialogues. "Most of us would much rather live with both hands if we can." Similarly, Jim Turner, coauthor of *Voice of the People*, defines transpartisan in terms of walking, "an action that integrates the right leg and the left. Walking is not a compromise between two legs; it is what makes forward motion possible."[14] In the same way, we have left and right eyes for better vision, and two ears for better hearing. The message from our own bodies is clear: two working together is more effective than one alone.

From this perspective, the historic choice between "stability" on the right and "change" on the left is not either/or but both/and. Do our bodies want stability? *Of course.* We want the temperature of our body to remain fairly constant at 98.6 degrees Fahrenheit. When it varies significantly, we become concerned. But do our bodies also want change? *Of course.* Just think how eager most of us were at the age of twelve or thirteen to grow taller and bigger. We didn't want our twelve-year-old bodies to stay the same. We wanted them to change, to mature, and to develop. If our bodies didn't change, we would once again go visit a doctor to find out what the cause—and cure— would be for arrested development, stunted growth, or failure to thrive.

We want our bodies to remain stable, not because we are conservatives but because we want a healthy metabolism. We want our bodies to progress, not because we are liberals but because we want to grow and develop.

This polarity, which each of us embodies, has been with us for hundreds of years and will be with us into the future. Managing that dynamic tension is a vital part of being a free citizen in a democracy.

The transpartisan perspective, then, *embraces* polarity. It embraces value *pairs* in a both/and framework—change and stability, liberty and authority, freedom and order, public service and free enterprise, secularism and sanctity. These pairs of values are not verbal weapons of political warfare. On the contrary, these contrasting values are poles of a paradox that democracy is designed to integrate.

To experience the absurdity of hyperpartisanship, let's try a thought experiment. Imagine that you were asked to select one value from each of these pairs. Which would you choose?

Change or stability?

Liberty or authority?

Freedom or order?

Public service or free enterprise?

Secularism or sanctity?

If we have difficulty or resist choosing one value or the other, it's only natural. These value pairs are two sides of a coin, two halves of a deeper truth, two poles that can be integrated. To bring Story #3 to life—that Americans can work together with people different from ourselves to find common ground—we need to recognize and, indeed, celebrate the connections between these pairs of values.

Most hyperpartisans on both the left and right have become unwitting sword wielders, blindly cutting the truth in half. They believe so strongly in their preferred value that they can no longer see the bigger picture. They endorse one of these words over the other when, in fact, the words are interdependent.

As we look at each of these pairs in turn, notice how serious—even fatal—the consequences can be if we cut the truth in half. Just recall, for instance, the biblical story about King Solomon's wisdom when dealing with two women who each claimed to be the mother of the same newborn baby. Dividing the baby between two women by cutting it in half would deprive both women of what they wanted and deprive the baby of life itself.

Similarly, when the left and right cut the truth in half, doing so ultimately kills the values that they both claim to stand for. The result is a political culture torn apart by competing values and devoid of common ground. Instead, the reuniting-America perspective honors both sets of values and strengthens our country.

We have already addressed change and stability, and concluded:

Change without stability becomes dangerous;
stability without change becomes stagnant.

So let's briefly examine the four other value pairs listed above. While there are obviously many more value polarities than these five, these are ones that almost always play a starring role in election-year showdowns.

Let's start with:

Liberty and Authority

The notion that liberty and authority are opposites, not complements, is clearly misguided. If we reflect for a moment, almost any liberty that we cherish depends on some kind of authority, regulations, ground rules, or established practices. These liberties depend on authorities, formal systems, or informal agreements that maintain them. For example, how long do we think we would have the liberty of driving a car if there were no rules of the road or if no entity repaired traffic lights and filled potholes? If no agency required driver's licenses and a minimum age or ensured that vehicles met certain basic standards of safety? We maintain the liberty of operating a motor vehicle precisely because of authority that preserves the liberty.

Similarly, even the liberty to walk in nature requires authority. Without a land-use authority, roads or homes or factories could be built anywhere, in any way. The liberty to stroll on a wild, untamed beach depends on some kind of authority to ensure that it remains wild.

Obviously, authority can be—and has been—abused. After all, America was founded in rebellion against colonial authority. Both authority and liberty, when not disciplined by the other, can quickly become undone.

Liberty without authority becomes license;
authority without liberty becomes domination.

Freedom and Order

The partisan quarrel between these two values is a dead-end. It makes no sense to honor one of them and dismiss the other. The transpartisan perspective, by contrast, is based on the simple premise that these polarities need to be thoughtfully managed, not resolved by cutting them in half.

As Lawrence Chickering observed years ago in his ground-breaking book *Beyond Left and Right: Breaking the Political Stalemate*, "order" and "freedom" are *both* conservative and liberal values. "I discovered that the apparently simple 'Left–Right' spectrum yielded so many contradictions that I couldn't keep up with them!" recalls this protégé of the renowned conservative activist William Buckley. "The truth is: the concepts of left and right conceal enormous conflict on both sides. So I embarked on a life-long quest to try to make sense of it."

Within the Democratic Party, there are disputes about these two values. Similarly, within the Republican Party there is constant infighting between the wing that favors freedom and the wing that favors order. Consider why Rand Paul, the libertarian senator from Kentucky, chose the University of California, Berkeley, historically the most liberal campus in America, as the site for his bold speech denouncing the internal threat of government surveillance of American citizens' e-mail and telephone communication. He did so during the national debate over the release of thousands of documents by former National Security Agency employee Edward Snowden. Paul was championing the conservative value of *freedom* (from government interference) in contrast to some other Republicans, who were championing *order* (obeying the law). Clearly, once again, freedom and order depend on the other if either value is to endure.

Freedom without order becomes anarchy;
order without freedom becomes dictatorship.

Public Service or Free Enterprise

It is astounding that in the twenty-first century, we are still fighting doggedly about the roles of the private and public sectors.

Let's start with two obviously one-sided examples from the
Democrats:

"If you've got a business, you didn't build that.
Somebody else made that happen."

—President Barack Obama

"Don't let anybody tell you that it's corporations
and businesses that create jobs."

—Presidential candidate Hillary Clinton

As quickly as they could, both of these liberal politicians
tried to correct their "misstatements." But the immediate backlash on Wall Street was harsh and strong. Clinton's statement,
for example, gave Republican presidential candidate Jeb Bush
an opportunity to express his shock at her "breathtaking" assertion. And it allowed other critics of Obama and Clinton to
pile on with comments attacking them for antibusiness bias.[15]

But if Democrats make ridiculous statements that sound
biased against free enterprise, Republicans make equally ludi-
crous comments that sound biased against government. Just
recall the mind-boggling comments about the economy from
2012 presidential hopeful Mitt Romney. He thought he was
speaking off the record to wealthy donors in Florida when he
said:

There are 47 percent of the people who will vote for
the president no matter what. All right, there are 47
percent who are with him, who are dependent upon
government, who believe that they are victims, who
believe the government has a responsibility to care for
them, who believe that they are entitled to health care,
to food, to housing, to you-name-it.[16]

Just as Obama and Clinton were quickly portrayed as "antibusiness," Romney was portrayed as "antigovernment." Unfortunately, the real issues they were both addressing were quickly distorted beyond recognition. Their admittedly sloppy statements were turned into nooses that partisans tried to put around the candidates' necks.

All this partisan jabbering results from an unwillingness to recognize the obvious transpartisan truth that both values—business and government—are vital parts of the American way of life. Government alone could never develop the Internet; business alone could never lead America to the moon. The question is not whether we need both, but rather what role each of them should play—and when.

> Public service without free enterprise goes bankrupt; free enterprise without public service loses its civic direction.

Secularism or Sanctity

Partisan game playing with religion offends transpartisans who, like the Founding Fathers, recognize that both secularism and sanctity have an honored place in American life.

"God" didn't appear in an inaugural speech until President James Monroe invoked the word in 1821. He promised that he would fulfill his presidential duties "with a firm reliance on the protection of Almighty God." Today, however, the vast majority of candidates for major office refer quite frequently and directly to God as if, somehow, they have received heavenly endorsement for their candidacy.[17]

In recent years, however, mentioning God has become so commonplace that it is now rare to find a prominent politician who makes a speech without invoking a higher power. Ronald

Reagan set a new record by invoking God in 96 percent of his speeches. Since then, it has become the norm for presidents, no matter what their party or their philosophy. George H. W. Bush did so almost as frequently (91 percent), as did Bill Clinton (93 percent) and George W. Bush (95 percent). While the data on President Obama's references to God is not complete, so far it seems he will not be far behind. In his second inaugural address, for example, Obama invoked God no less than five times. The trend has become solidly bipartisan and, if anything, on the rise.[18]

Given what pollsters say about the voting public, this steady drumbeat of references to the divine is not surprising. Polls consistently show that the overwhelming majority of Americans believe in God. One recent survey uncovered growing numbers of voters who want politicians to pray in public and for their clergy to endorse candidates.[19] As George Gallup Jr. put it, "So many people in the country say they believe in God that it seems unnecessary to even conduct surveys on the question."[20] (Although those who check "none" when asked to identify their religious affiliation are the fastest-growing group, they are still a small minority.[21])

From a transpartisan perspective, politicians can say "God" (or "Jehovah" or "Allah") whenever they want. They can honor the divine in their speeches, ask for his help, thank the Creator, or even make the patriotic request that God "bless America." If sincere rather than mechanical, these invocations of higher power can be genuinely spiritually uplifting. But there is a difference between *worshipping* God and *using* God for partisan purposes.

The issue is the boundary line between a place of worship and civic space. When we cross that border, sanctity and secularism encounter each other and must find common ground. Our private faith (religious sanctity) and mutual respect (civic secularism) can coexist. As Michael Cromartie, vice president of the Ethics and Public Policy Center, delicately advises his fellow religious conservatives, "It is urgent that you learn to speak in a public language of mutual respect and civic pluralism, not a private language of revelation and faith."[22]

> Secularism without the sacred can become hollow and commercial; sanctity without secularism becomes exclusive and dogmatic.

UNCOVERING THE UNITY
THAT CONNECTS US ALL

Each of these pairs of partisan values leads many Americans to the same *trans*partisan conclusion. One is not right and the other wrong. Both need to be integrated with the other to forge a sustainable approach. Just as a good parent would never choose discipline instead of love (or vice versa), so we as citizens in a democracy would never choose order instead of freedom (or vice versa). Instead, we seek a sound, integrated relationship between them that enhances our life, liberty, and pursuit of happiness.

At the heart of the transpartisan movement, then, is a commitment to integrating, not polarizing, core American values. Doing so will enable us to nurture a healthy relationship with our adversaries and to identify the best ideas from across the *entire* political spectrum. The result of honoring these pairs of values will be a leaner and wiser government and a healthier, more civil political culture. As the Bipartisan Policy Center's 2014 Annual Report puts it, there is room for both partisanship *and* collaboration, the many and the one, *pluribus* and *unum*.

As evidenced by the scores of remarkable organizations profiled in this book, we Americans know how to design systems that transcend "liberal" and "conservative" labels. Independent-minded Americans who want our democracy to work better have launched these initiatives. These pioneers from across the political spectrum are working together—to build bridges, not walls; to heal, not poison; to solve problems, not exploit them. They are restoring the healthy relationship between *pluribus* and *unum*. For many of us today, they are true American heroes.

But these heroes are not utopians; they are practical, every-day change-makers rooted in hard civic and economic realities. Liberal-leaning leaders in the blue states must literally *see the light*: they cannot flourish without the red states' energy resources. Similarly, the conservative-leaning leaders in the red states literally need to *wise up*: their economies cannot flourish without the blue states' knowledge industries. Whether we admit it or not, red and blue states need each other to strengthen and reunite America.

Of course, no single reform, and no single organization, can turn a hyperpartisan attack culture into a transpartisan problem-solving paradise. But, taken together, the people and organizations profiled in this book are catalyzing a profound turnaround. They prove that we, the people, know how to make democracy work.

So when you and I contribute our energy, our money, or our vote, let us invest them wisely. Our actions and resources can reinforce the divisive, destructive hyperpartisan trance—or we can wake up and become active, patriotic citizens of the Reunited States.

The choice is yours, and mine, and every American's.

HOW WE CAN
BRIDGE THE
PARTISAN DIVIDE

WE AMERICANS ARE famous around the world for our amazing inventiveness and creative ingenuity. Silicon Valley, Hollywood, and Wall Street are more than zip codes; they are global icons. Technical triumphs (witness the iPhone), cultural blockbusters (think of *Star Wars* or *Titanic*), and corporate innovation sweep unstoppably across the world. At our best, the United States continues to inspire humanity with our core values of justice and freedom. What we have to do now is apply this ingenuity to our own democracy.

Instead of complaining about what *they* should do to fix what's wrong, it's far more empowering and energizing to ask what *we ourselves* can do to bridge the partisan divide. Here are ten steps that many of our fellow citizens, including my colleagues and me, are taking to bridge the partisan divide.

Perhaps you are involved in one or more of these activities; if so, you are part of this movement already. If not, please notice which of them inspire you to take action yourself—or start a bridging initiative of your own!

STEP 1:
TAKE A TRANSPARTISAN
VACATION

We all have our partisan identities. Some of us simply call ourselves "conservative" or "liberal." Others have more nuanced labels like "libertarian," or "social liberal, fiscal conservative," or "progressive." But whatever our political identity is, we have usually been living at that political address for a long time.

I invite you to join me in taking a vacation from our regular identities. Take a week off, or even a month. Experience our country afresh. You have everything to gain and nothing to lose because—remember!—it is only a vacation. You can always return home and, as you would a comfortable set of clothes in the closet, put your political identity back on again.

Just think about the rewards of even a short vacation away from the land of left and right.

- You will enjoy some well-earned time off from defending all of your old positions against those who disagree.

- You may broaden your own perspective and possibly learn how to communicate your views more effectively to those with whom you differ.

- Your vacation may refresh you enough that you feel like taking a longer one.

STEP 2:
RECOGNIZE AND EXERCISE
YOUR LIBERTY TO LEARN

An inmate in a prison cell can be freed by a guard. But if we are in a prison of our own mind-set, only we can set ourselves free. Thankfully, we are blessed in America to have the external freedoms that are still rare in many parts of the world. But to benefit from those freedoms, we require the inner freedom of learning—and unlearning.

To do so, we need to think for ourselves—which is easier said than done. Generations of Americans have worked, fought, and sometimes died for our hard-won freedoms. But it's up to each of us to make sure that we use them.

On some issues, we can rely on our own firsthand experience. But on other issues, we have no choice but to rely on second-hand information, whether it comes from friends, teachers, news channels, websites, social media, etc. Can we be absolutely sure that the information we are receiving is true and complete?

Unless we have an infallible news source, we must cross-check. Just as we may seek a doctor's second opinion when facing a critical medical choice, so we can naturally seek a second—or even a third—opinion about a controversial public issue that deeply concerns us.

After participating in one of our Transpartisan Leadership 101 seminars, a young woman just completing her freshman year in college approached me, glowing with excitement. "I came into college thinking, 'I'm a Democrat,'" she said. "'My parents are Democrats,' I thought, 'and this is what I am; I can't be anything else.' But then I was hit with so many different political views and opinions that I felt like I wasn't a Democrat anymore. I felt like I'd lost my political identity, but didn't know what to do about it. And then coming to the event today showed me that there is a place that I can belong in politics—a place where I can think for myself."[1]

I was touched by how this student was fully exercising her liberty to learn. Some of us grew up in households, for example, hearing that America is always right and never makes a mistake in the world. Others of us grew up in families that were so critical of America that the country was always described as a bully or an oppressor. In both cases, if we want to grow up to be free, we will have to unlearn the simple half-truths we were taught and develop the discernment to decide *for ourselves* when America's actions at home and abroad are virtuous—and when they are not.

Always praising America is not patriotism. It is idolatry. But always criticizing America is not patriotism, either. It is ingratitude. The former is blind to America's faults; the latter is blind to America's virtues. Truly loving our country requires independent-minded thinking and lifelong learning—which are both at the very heart of the movement to reunite America.

STEP 3:
GET INVOLVED OUTSIDE
YOUR RED OR BLUE BOX

No matter how conservative or liberal our upbringing may have been, we are free to step out of that box. To do so, however, we need to wake up from what conservative columnist David Brooks calls the trance of "partyism." According to him, partyism is becoming the new form of racism: we arguably are discriminating against our fellow Americans because of their party label more than their skin color.[2]

Whether we were born white and Protestant in New Hampshire, black and Muslim in Chicago, Hispanic and Catholic in Albuquerque, or Jewish and secular in New York City, we are free to cross whatever religious, racial, or geographic boundaries we want. Just as we are free to cross state lines without a passport, we are free to cross the political spectrum without asking anyone's permission. No one has the right to stop us from getting involved in any legal activity or philosophy or educational experience that attracts us. Of course there are practical constraints. Money can be an obstacle. So can race or religion. But beyond those limitations, we are free to step out of the identity that others impose on us and assert our own uniqueness.

"Fight for Technicolor," says Laura Chasin, whom we met in chapter 2. Now in her mid-seventies, she explains her memorable phrase this way: "Don't reduce everyone and everything to black-and-white. Stand up for the multicolored reality of yourself and others."

Sometimes taking black-and-white partisan stands on certain issues may make sense. But before you take the divisive partisan road, please think twice. If you feel one side is completely right and the other is completely wrong, then a partisan approach is sensible. If you and your colleagues, acting as partisans, can achieve your objectives in an effective and enduring manner, go for it. However, if this is not the case, then it is unlikely that partisanship—particularly aggressive, bitter hyperpartisanship—is your best bet. When your adversary or other stakeholders can undermine your hard-own achievement, being transpartisan will get you further than being hyperpartisan.

STEP 4:
IDENTIFY AND SUPPORT LEADERS
WHO ARE REUNITING AMERICA

It's not hard to blindly "get involved." These days it takes little more than a tap on our cellphone to claim that we are an "active citizen." But what is the quality of our involvement? What is the impact of our engagement?

Over the years, Debilyn Molineaux has worked with many of the leaders of organizations in this field, ranging from Living Room Conversations to the Coffee Party to the Bridge Alliance. Her career as a bridge builder began when she was a candidate for office with advisers who were Democrats, Republicans, and Greens. The experience of running for office awakened her to the need for a new kind of collaboration in public life.

"Having worked with so many visionaries and their organizations," says Molineaux, "I have met a lot of high-altitude leaders. The ones who inspire me are those who put their visions into practice—whose feet are firmly on the ground. Once we get down to earth, we can find the path forward together."

One of the best ways to recognize these leaders who walk their talk is to ask ourselves:

- *Does this leader listen?* I don't mean listening for show. I mean actually listening because he or she wants to learn. Does he or she take time to pay genuine attention and ask thoughtful questions?

- *Does this leader work with diverse partners or teams?* Because transpartisan leaders are bridge builders, they need someone on the other side of the divide to help complete the bridge. That's why a Van Jones teams up with a Newt Gingrich to reform the criminal justice system, or a Democrat partners with a Republican in the House of Representatives to push through a vital piece of legislation. They know that a partnership of opposites or a team that is diverse will be more likely to gain the trust of all stakeholders.

■ *Does this leader treat his or her adversaries with respect?* Those who are reuniting America may criticize the behavior of a corporation, a political party, or an organization. But even if they are confronting corruption or other serious wrongdoing, these leaders allow their adversaries to maintain their dignity. They have learned to be hard on the issue and soft on the people—not because they are trying to be nice, but because they are determined to be effective.

■ *Does this leader's presence increase trust and collaboration?* We have all been in meetings or public events where the actions of the leaders decreased trust. By contrast, bridging the divide requires catalyzing an environment that is safe, respectful, and attentive to the feelings of those who are present. When transpartisans lead, trust is raised, and the capacity to collaborate is enhanced.

STEP 5:
JOIN A BRIDGE-BUILDING
INITIATIVE—OR START YOUR OWN

Sometimes you can *follow* the leader, but other times you have to *become* a leader.

Most of the organizations profiled in these pages were started by people just like you and me. Even if they did not have relevant professional credentials, a particular skill, or enough money, they still felt called to step in—and they did.

You may want to join an existing organization or, like many of the pioneers profiled in part 1, start your own. But whichever you choose, remember: You are now a Founding Father or Founding Mother. You are (re)inventing the (re)United States of America.

Like any other emergent movement, the movement to re-unite America does not have one leader or one headquarters. But you know enough now to find your own path to being a bridge builder. To learn more, attend a Citizen University gathering and listen to a wide range of leaders; or check out which of the thousands of organizations in the National Coalition for Dialogue & Deliberation are in your area; or consult the growing roster of bridge-building initiatives in the Bridge Alliance.

And if this research uncovers no existing organization that appeals to you, reach out to your neighbors. Form a "red-white-and-blue" (Democratic-Independent-Republican) team and tackle a local problem or focus on a local opportunity. Together, you can put Story #3—Americans working together—into action right in your own backyard.

STEP 6:
MAKE SURE THE RULES PROMOTE
FAIRNESS AND FREEDOM

It's neither the losing party nor even the winning party that has the ultimate power. The power is with those who make and enforce the rules of the game. So before you decide to join Team A or Team B, examine the rules.

When it comes to football, we all know that the big salaries and the big news stories will be about the hotshot quarterbacks or wide receivers, not the referees. But when it comes to real life in a democracy, the refs matter more than we know. They determine whether the field is level and the boundary lines clearly marked. They make sure that the players are on the field, the spectators are in the stands, and no one is throwing bottles or interfering with the game. They call the fouls, set the penalties, and ensure that the game is conducted in a way that safeguards and strengthens it for future generations. Ultimately, they are the ones who determine whether this fragile invention called democracy is going to flourish or decay.

So don't immediately assume that you want to play on one team or another. You might want to become an official who keeps the game honest and brings out the best in *all* the players.

STEP 7:
VOTE FOR BRIDGE-BUILDING
CANDIDATES

When election time comes, we check one box or another, or we don't vote at all. Since there is no place to check "transpartisan" on Election Day, we must choose for whom to vote: Republican, Democrat, Independent, Green, Libertarian, etc. Whatever we choose (or refuse to choose), we have made a partisan choice.

But aren't we all more than that?

When we think about our daily lives, most of us are (or want to be) citizens of the *United* States of America. We pay taxes to a *federal* government. We drive our cars on roads with *common* laws and with a driver's license issued by *government* officials. Many of our children go to *public* schools. We all use currency issued by the US Treasury. So, no matter how partisan we may be, we are living every day in a reality that is based on what we share, not only on how we differ.

We naturally prefer a candidate who agrees with us on our hot-button issues. It's only human to want to see our favorite win on Election Day. But something else is at stake today, something equally important. It is reflected in the advice that generations of parents have given to their children: "It's not whether you win or lose, but how you play the game."

If you want to support candidates who are good for the game of democracy, here are a handful of ways you can recognize them:

- They avoid "spin," are honest, and express their genuine, heartfelt truth.

- They listen to voters and citizen groups, not just deep-pocket donors and lobbyists.

- They maintain their independence of thought regardless of party membership.

- They resist toxic partisan attacks and engage in cross-party problem solving.

- They identify real challenges to the American Dream and propose thoughtful solutions.

- They bring religion into their campaign (if at all) with genuine reverence.

- They reflect the highest values of our country and make us proud to be Americans.

STEP 8:
CONNECT WITH OTHER
BOUNDARY-CROSSING CITIZENS

For dyed-in-the-wool liberals or conservatives, it is easy to find your tribe. From the Internet to TV channels, it doesn't take long to connect with those who share your partisan worldview. But if you are not in one of those two camps, it can often be harder to find like-minded souls.

Given the rapid growth of bridge-building efforts, however, you will find transpartisans at work near where you live. They may be hosting living room conversations across the divide. They may be fostering dialogues in your place of worship, your local library, or your community center. They may be business leaders who are sitting down to solve problems that public officials can't handle. They may also be in your state legislature, where Democrats, Republicans, and Independents are teaming up to tackle tough issues. They may even be on Capitol Hill, stepping across the aisle and partnering with a partisan adversary to get something done.

To find others who want to be free from the red-or-blue box, it makes sense for us to create a space where those of us who want to learn from everyone across the spectrum can find each other. In addition to a quadrennial convention for the Democratic Party and the Republican Party, we need a convention for America.

In my life, as I witnessed twelve pairs of party conventions, they seemed to increasingly resemble football pep rallies at rival high schools. Instead of just the true-blue Democrats gathering in one city and all the red-hot Republicans gathering in another, we need to establish a Citizens' Summit where Americans of contrasting opinions gather to learn from their differences and find common ground.[3]

Remember: The goal is not to create another box. It's about building a space that is "red, white, and blue"—a place in our democracy where we can *all* sit down together.

STEP 9:
PLAY BY THE (GOLDEN) RULES

No matter what your faith tradition may be, it probably has a version of the Golden Rule. While the wording differs, the major world religions are united in encouraging their believers to treat others with the same consideration and care that one would like to be treated with. Whether you are Christian ("All things whatsoever ye would that others should do to you, do ye so to them"), Jewish ("What is hateful to you, do not do to your fellow man"), or Muslim ("No one of you is a believer until he desires for his brother that which he desires for himself"), the rule is clear.[4]

The question is: will we practice what we preach?

The Faith and Politics Institute on Capitol Hill asks the members of Congress who participate in its programs to practice their "Call to Prayer." Based on their belief that "people of faith have a responsibility to show respect for others of different views," they ask politicians to pledge that during the campaign season they will do the following: "Practice respectful dialogue by applying the Golden Rule in political discussions."

This does not mean assuming that others think just like us or that they want exactly what we want. The rules mean that we need to respect their uniqueness just as we want them to respect ours. With respect comes trust, with trust comes new possibilities, and with new possibilities comes hope.

STEP 10:
HOLD BOTH LOVE AND POWER
IN YOUR HANDS

All of the preceding nine steps have something in common: they challenge us to combine our capacity to connect and love with our desire for control and power. Fortunately, each of us has two hands. If we hold love in one and power in the other, we can help bridge the partisan divide.

"Power without love is reckless and abusive, and love without power is sentimental and anemic," Reverend Martin

Luther King Jr. said a half-century ago. But far less often cited is his next sentence: "Power at its best is love implementing the demands of justice, and justice at its best is power correcting everything that stands against love."[5] This means fixing systems that breed indifference or injustice. It means challenging campaign practices that bring out the worst, not the best, in those daring souls who truly want to serve the public. It means changing rules that foster hate.

"The thrill of political hating," as columnist David Brooks put it recently, must give way to the thrill of political loving.[6] We must love our country so deeply, and with such devotion, that our internal "enemies" once again become fellow citizens, and perhaps one day allies or even friends. The soul of our democracy depends on it.

If all of us do our part, our chorus of commitment to our country will cut through the hyperpartisan static. We will then hear more clearly than ever before the unique harmony that is America the beautiful.

NOTES

Preface

1. David Brooks, "Donald Trump's Allure: Ego as Ideology," *New York Times*, August 4, 2015, A27, http://www.nytimes .com/2015/08/04/opinion/david-brooks-trumps-allure-ego -as-ideology.html?_r=0.

2. Seventy percent of millennials and 90 percent of baby boomers say they are "very patriotic." Katie Reilly, "A generational gap in American patriotism," Pew Research Center, *Fact Tank*, July 3, 2013, http://www.pewresearch.org/fact-tank/2013/07/03/a -generational-gap-in-american-patriotism/.

Introduction

1. *Political Polarization in the American Public: How Increasingly Ideological Uniformity and Partisan Antipathy Affect Politics, Compromise and Everyday Life*, Pew Research Center, U.S. Politics & Policy, June 12, 2014, http://www.people-press.org/2014/06/12/ political-polarization -in-the-american-public/.

2. Special DYG (Daniel Yankelovich Group) SCAN Study, May 12, 1995, titled "The Public's Views about the Current 'Moral Crisis,'" cited in Daniel Yankelovich, *The Magic of Dialogue: Transforming Conflict into Cooperation* (New York: Simon and Schuster, 1999).

3. *Nonpartisan*: maintaining that one is not taking sides with either of the two major parties but is somehow neutral. *Bipartisan*: supporting the two major parties to negotiate a compromise. *Postpartisan*: imagining that one is now living, or will one day live, in a country without partisan divisions.

4. Remarks by John Haidt, "Conclave on Polarization," Big Sur, California, October 6, 2014, quoted in Steve McIntosh, "Reflections on Esalen's 2014 Conclave on Political Polarization," *Institute for Cultural Revolution Blog*, October 14, 2014, accessed

November 6, 2015, http://www.culturalevolution.org/blog/
reflections-on-esalens-2014-conclave-on-political-polarization/#
.Vj0N5KanCkQ.

5. Yankelovich, Special DYG SCAN Study.

6. Ibid.

7. Bipartisan Policy Center, "Taking the Poison Out of Partisanship," conference, Tulane University, November 9, 2009, http://
bipartisanpolicy.org/events/taking-poison-out-partisanship/.

8. Alan Abramowitz and Steven Webster, "The Only Thing We
Have to Fear Is the Other Party," Sabato's Crystal Ball, Center
for Politics, June 4, 2015, as cited in Joan Blades and Ralph
Benko, "How Radically to Uproot the Root of Our Political
Misery," Huffington Post, June 17, 2015, accessed July 3, 2015,
http://www.huffingtonpost.com/living-room-conversations/
how-radically-to-uproot-t_b_7604412.html.

9. Mark Gerzon, *A House Divided: Six Belief Systems Struggling for
America's Soul* (New York: Tarcher, 1996).

10. Thomas L. Friedman, "Bonfire of the Assets, With Trump
Lighting Matches," *New York Times*, August 26, 2015, http://
www.nytimes.com/2015/08/26/opinion/thomas-friedman
-bonfire-of-the-assets-with-trump-lighting-matches.html?_r=0.

Chapter 1. Reinventing Citizenship

1. "Figure 1: U.S. 8th Graders Scoring 'Proficient' or Higher on
the National Assessment of Educational Progress by Subject,"
in Robert Pondiscio et al., *Shortchanging the Future: The Crisis of
History and Civics in American Schools*, Pioneer Institute White
Paper, no. 100 (April 2013).

2. Robert Pondiscio, "Let's Set a National Standard for Our Students—a Really Low One," *Atlantic*, April 2013.

3. Comments by Dana Bash at a conference hosted by No Labels "National Ideas Meeting" at the United States Institute of
Peace, Washington, DC, September 17, 2014.

4. Brooks Jackson and Kathleen Hall Jamieson, *unSpun: Finding Facts in a World of Disinformation* (New York: Random House, 2007).

5. Connie Cass, "Poll: Confused by Issues of the Day? Join the Club," AP Big Story, September 27, 2014, accessed July 23, 2015, http://bigstory.ap.org/article/356e4efefb204b10b2330 ac28d7a03eb/poll-confused-issues-day-join-club.

6. "Jabbing at Republican Rivals, Jeb Bush Calls for Civility," *New York Times*, July 28, 2015.

7. Chris Cillizza, "Bernie Sanders's Liberty University speech, annotated," *Washington Post*, September 14, 2015, http://www.washingtonpost.com/news/the-fix/wp/2015/09/14/bernie-sanders-liberty-university-speech-annotated/#.

8. Jonathan Gould, ed., *Guardian of Democracy: The Civic Mission of Schools* (New York: Carnegie Corporation of New York and the Center for Information and Research on Civic Learning and Engagement, 2003).

9. Mabel McKinney Browning, interview by author via phone, May 2015.

10. From "Transpartisan Practices: Michael Ostrolenk," YouTube video, https://www.youtube.com/watch?v=ju9IzNtJi4A.

11. Robert E. Slavin, *Educational Research in an Age of Accountability* (New York: Pearson, 2006).

12. Ibid.

13. Sworn-Again America, Citizen University and Carnegie Corporation of New York, accessed August 6, 2015, http://www.swornagainamerica.us/.

14. The retreat was hosted by Reuniting America, a project then under the direction of Joseph McCormick, with pivotal assistance from Michael Ostolenk, John Steiner, and a much wider team of colleagues. Aspen Wye Institute, Maryland, September 18-21, 2007.

15. For a more detailed analysis, see Chris Ernst and Jeffrey Yip, "Case Study/Mark Gerzon—Breaking down boundaries in the climate change debate," *Leadership in Action* 29, issue 3 (July/August 2009): 12-16, http://onlinelibrary.wiley.com/ doi/10.1002/lia.1292/abstract.

Chapter 2. Leading beyond Borders

1. From remarks made at the "Conclave on Polarization," Esalen Institute, October 2014.

2. The Anti-Defamation League, letter to MSNBC, July 28, 2006, http://archive.adl.org/media_watch/tv/20060728-msnbc .html#.VSO5Lij9l74.

3. Adam Nagourney, "To Voters, Washington Is Biggest Loser," *New York Times*, November 5, 2014.

4. Mark Gerzon, "Fighting Words," *Washington Post*, October 16, 1996, accessed August 3, 2015, http://www .washingtonpost.com/archive/opinions/1996/10/16/ fighting-words/02fec312-88e7-4831-a82f-9c4a4a99097b/.

5. Barack Obama, "Remarks by the President on Economic Mobility," December 4, 2013, the White House, https:// www.whitehouse.gov/the-press-office/2013/12/04/ remarks-president-economic-mobility.

6. Jackson and Jamieson, *unSpun*.

7. Gretchen Morgenson and Joshua Rosner, *Reckless Endangerment: How Outsized Ambition, Greed, and Corruption Created the Worst Financial Crisis of Our Time* (New York: Times Books, 2011).

8. Nicholas Kristof, "The American Dream Is Leaving America," *New York Times*, October 28, 2014.

9. Jonathan Weisman, "At Global Economic Meeting, US Primacy Is Seen as Ebbing," *New York Times*, April 17, 2015.

10. Gail Collins, "A Man with a Plan," *New York Times*, September 11, 2014.

11. Howard Schultz, chairman and CEO of Starbucks, interview by Charlie Rose, *Charlie Rose*, PBS, April 10, 2014.

12. Howard Schultz, "America Deserves a Servant Leader," *New York Times*, August 6, 2015.

13. From a conversation with the author, May 2014.

14. Laura Chasin, "How to Break the Argument Habit," *Christian Science Monitor*, October 26, 2004, accessed August 6, 2015, http://www.csmonitor.com/2004/1026/p08s01-coop.html.

15. Comments from Laura Chasin in a series of interviews, spring 2015.

16. Remarks at a meeting celebrating his election, in Springfield, Illinois, on November 20, 1960. http://genius.com/Abraham-lincoln-the-papers-and-writings-of-abraham-lincoln-vol-v-chap-327-annotated.

17. This and the following quotes are from an interview with Heierbacher by Jack Becker of the Kettering Foundation, March 14, 2014, https://www.kettering.org/blogs/connecting-communities-sandy-heierbacher-national-coalition-dialogue-deliberation.

18. Living Room Conversations, http://www.livingroomconversations.org.

19. Glenn Davis, "The Village Square: Political Opposites Break Bread over Civil Discourse," IVN, April 1, 2014, accessed November 9, 2014, http://ivn.us/2014/04/01/village-square-political-opposites-break-bread-civil-discourse/.

20. Quotes from Desloge and Katz are from Karl Etters, "The Village Square expands to other cities," *Tallahassee Democrat*, June 21, 2014, accessed February 13, 2015, http://www.tallahassee.com/story/news/local/2014/06/21/village-square-expands-cities/11230415/.

21. The other stories are available at Everyday Democracy, http://www.everyday-democracy.org/stories/change.

22. Sarah Pulliam, "Richard Cizik Resigns from the National Association of Evangelicals," *Christianity Today*, December 11, 2008, accessed July 25, 2015, http://www.christianitytoday.com/ct/2008/decemberweb-only/150-42.0.html.

23. For more information about Cizik, watch his interview with Bill Moyers. Richard Cizik, interview by Bill Moyers, "Understanding Our Connection to Nature," *Moyers & Company*, October 4, 2013.

24. Ostrolenk's entire speech is available in "Transpartisan Visions: Michael Ostrolenk in 2014," YouTube video, posted by Mediators Foundation, June 6, 2014, https://www.youtube.com/watch?v=jwUvO7348kU.

25. Ecclesiastes 4:9–12.

Chapter 3. Championing the Whole Truth

1. Neena Satija, "On Climate, a Younger Bush's Ideas Stray From Party Ideology," *New York Times*, August 30, 2014.

2. Jessamyn Conrad, *What You Should Know About Politics . . . but Don't: A Nonpartisan Guide to the Issues That Matter*, 2nd ed. (New York: Arcade Publishing, 2012).

3. "Newt Gingrich and Van Jones Live," *Huffington Post Live*, April 1, 2015, http://www.msn.com/en-us/video/news/newt-gingrich-and-van-jones-live/vp-AAakqkD.

4. Correspondence with the author from Joan Blades, who cochaired the Coalition meeting with Debilyn Molineaux, president of the Coffee Party.

5. Bill Shireman, *Toward a New Agenda for America* (San Francisco: Future 500 Publishing, 2012).

6. Aakif Ahmad, "Turning disagreements into solutions—fixing gridlock," TEDxFoggyBottom, accessed January 28, 2014, https://www.youtube.com/watch?v=jponklwO1os.

7. The study analyzed questions from dozens of surveys from numerous sources, including the American National Election Studies, Pew, major media outlets, the Chicago Council

on Global Affairs, and the Program for Public Consultation. Responses were analyzed based on whether the respondents lived in red or blue districts or states. *A Not So Divided America: Is the Public as Polarized as Congress, or Are Red and Blue Districts Pretty Much the Same?* (Washington, DC: Voice of the People and Program for Public Consultation, July 2, 2014).

8. Andrew Moylan, "Defending America, Defending Taxpayers," R Street Institute, June 4, 2013, http://rstreet.org/policy-study/defending-america-defending-taxpayers/.

9. Robert M. Gates, "Remarks on Eisenhower Library (Defense Spending), Abilene, Kansas, May 8, 2010," US Department of Defense, accessed March 11, 2014, http://archive.defense.gov/speeches/speech.aspx?speechid=1467.

10. Associated Press, "Tom Coburn outlines $68 billion in defense cuts," *Politico*, November 15, 2012, http://www.politico.com/story/2012/11/tom-coburn- outlines-68-billion-in-defense-cuts-083910.

11. Developed by Mark Gerzon/Mediators Foundation in collaboration with ChoicePoint Consulting, the Public Conversation Project, Passageworks Institute, and other partners.

12. Mark McKinnon, interview by author, *Brown Spectator*, May 8, 2011, http://brown-spectator.com/2011/05/no-labels-interview/.

Chapter 4. Serving the People

1. "Partisan Polarization Surges in Bush, Obama Years: Trends in American Values: 1987–2012," Pew Research Center, Washington, DC (June 4, 2012), http://www.people-press.org/2012/06/04/partisan-polarization-surges-in-bush-obama-years/.

2. Evidence abounds for this assertion. For an excellent summary, see Mickey Edwards's *The Parties Versus the People: How to Turn Republicans and Democrats into Americans* (New Haven, CT: Yale University Press, 2012), chapter 6, "Government Leaders, Not Party Leaders."

3. Michael Grunwald, *The New New Deal: The Hidden Story of Change in the Obama Era* (New York: Simon & Schuster, 2012).

4. Charles M. Blow, "The Obama Opposition," *New York Times*, November 10, 2014.

5. Nagourney, "To Voters, Washington Is Biggest Loser."

6. Blow, "The Obama Opposition."

7 Charlotte Alter, "Voter Turnout in Midterm Elections Hits 72-Year Low," *Time*, November 10, 2014.

8. Boris Shor, "How U.S. State Legislatures Are Polarized and Getting More Polarized (in 2 graphs)," *Washington Post*, "Monkey Cage," January 14, 2014, http://www.washingtonpost.com/blogs/monkey-cage/wp/2014/01/14/how-u-s-state-legisla tures-are-polarized-and-getting-more-polarized-in-2-graphs/.

9. Quoted in Edwards, *The Parties Versus the People*, 159.

10. Brian Montopoli, "Should Partisans Be in Charge of Our Elections?" *CBS News*, September 27, 2012, http://www.cbsnews .com/news/should-partisans-be-in-charge-of-our-elections/.

11. "Conclave on Polarization," Big Sur, California, October 6, 2014. Steve McIntosh, "Reflections on Esalen's 2014 Conclave on Political Polarization," *Institute for Cultural Revolution Blog*, October 14, 2014, accessed July 22, 2015, http://www.cultura levolution.org/blog/reflections-on-esalens-2014-conclave-on -political-polarization/#.VbBYCqRVhBc.

12. Quoted in "Should partisans be in charge of our elections?" Brian Montopoli, *CBS News*, September 27, 2012.

13. Jill Colvin, "The Perma-Campaign: For Bill de Blasio, the Race Never Ends," *Observer*, February 4, 2014, http://observer. com/2014/02/the-perma-campaign-for-bill-de-blasio-the-race-never-ends/.

14. Nicholas Confessore and Eric Lichtblau, "'Campaigns' Aren't Necessarily Campaigns in the Age of 'Super PACs,'" *New York Times*, May 17, 2015, http://www.nytimes.com/2015/05/18/us/politics/super-pacs-are-remaking-16-campaigns-official-or -not.html.

15. Eric Lichtblau, "F.E.C. Can't Curb 2016 Election Abuse, Commission Chief Says," *New York Times*, May 2, 2015, http://www .nytimes.com/2015/05/03/us/politics/fec-cant-curb-2016-elec tion-abuse-commission-chief-says.html.

16. Tamera Luzzatto, conversation with the author.

17. Joseph E. Stiglitz, "A Tax System Stacked Against the 99 Percent," *New York Times*, "Opinionator," April 14, 2013, http:// opinionator.blogs.nytimes.com/2013/04/14/a-tax-system -stacked-against-the-99-percent/?_r=0.

18. Quotes are taken from the website of Open Debates, one of the most effective critics of the Commission on Presidential Debates.

19. Barack Obama, "Remarks at Signing of the Defending Public Safety Employees' Retirement Act and the Trade Preferences Extension Act of 2015, June 29, 2015," the White House, https://www.whitehouse.gov/the-press-office/2015/06/29/ remarks-president-signing-defending-public-safety-employees -retirement.

20. Frank Luntz, "The Midterms Were Not a Republican Revolution," *New York Times*, November 5, 2014, accessed August 6, 2015, http://www.nytimes.com/2014/11/06/opinion/the-mid terms-were-not-a-republican-revolution.html?_r=0.

21. For a comprehensive overview of these reforms, see Edwards, *The Parties Versus the People*; Linda Killian's *The Swing Vote: The Untapped Power of Independents* (New York: St. Martin's Press, 2012); and Norman Ornstein and Thomas Mann's *It's Even Worse Than It Looks: How the American Constitutional System Collided with the New Politics of Extremism* (New York: Basic Books, 2012).

22. Carolyn J. Lukensmeyer, *Bringing Citizen Voices to the Table: A Guide for Public Managers* (San Francisco: Jossey-Bass, 2012).

23. Julie Bosman, "Scott Walker Proposes Shutting Wisconsin Ethics Board," *New York Times*, July 21, 2015, http://www.nytimes .com/2015/07/21/us/scott-walker-proposes-shutting-wiscon sin-ethics-board.html.

24. Karen Hobert Flynn, "Scott Walker's War on Good Government," *Daily Beast*, February 8, 2015, http://www
.thedailybeast.com/articles/2015/02/08/scott-walker-s-war
-on-good-government.html.

25. Jacqueline Salit, "Are voting rights for all voters? Let's ask Hillary," *Arizona Republic*, June 27, 2015, http://
www.azcentral.com/story/opinion/op-ed/2015/06/28/
voting-rights-hillary-clinton/29297871/.

26. From a speech delivered in March 2015 in New York City at the meeting hosted by IndependentVoting.org.

27. "The Solution to Fixing Dysfunction in Congress," John K. Delaney, *Washington Post*, September 2, 2014, https://www.
washingtonpost.com/opinions/the-solution-to-fixing-dys
function-in-congress/2014/09/02/0f0d0a9a-31e6-11e4-9e92
-0899b306bbea_story.html.

28. Charles E. Schumer, "End Partisan Primaries, Save America," *New York Times*, July 21, 2014, http://www.nytimes
.com/2014/07/22/opinion/charles-schumer-adopt-the-open
-primary.html?_r=0.

29. Burstein quotes taken from "David Burstein: Run for America," YouTube video, posted by poptech, November 5, 2014, http://
www.youtube.com/watch?v=CWIYdnt6X2Q; and Aaron Sankin, "One millennial's quest to save Washington, one race at a time," *Kernel*, "Daily Dot," March 8, 2015, http://kernelmag
.dailydot.com/issue-sections/headline-story/12070/run-for
-america-david-burstein/#sthash.lnoTeJ9p.dpuf.

30. Pew Research Center Social & Demographic Trends, "Millennials: Unmoored from Institutions," March 5, 2014, http://www
.pewsocialtrends.org/2014/03/07/millennials-in-adulthood/
sdt-next-america-03-07-2014-0-01/.

31. Cited in Edwards, *The Parties Versus the People*, 171.

32. Ibid., 172.

33. Mickey Edwards, "Politics of the Future," *Aspen Idea*, Summer 2005, http://www.aspeninstitute.org/sites/default/files/
content/docs/rodel/rodelideaarticle.pdf.

34. Ibid.

35. Jason Grumet, *City of Rivals: Restoring the Glorious Mess of American Democracy* (Guilford, CT: Lyons Press, 2014).

Chapter 5. Born out of Crisis

1. Quoted by Arthur C. Brooks, president of the American Enterprise Institute, "The Thrill of Political Hating," *New York Times*, June 8, 2015, http://www.nytimes.com/2015/06/08/opinion/the-thrill-of-political-hating.html?_r=0.

2. Matthew 12:25, New King James Version.

3. Jeffrey M. Jones, "Record-High 42% of Americans Identify as Independents," *Gallup Politics*, January 8, 2014, http://www.gallup.com/poll/166763/record-high-americans-identify-independents.aspx.

4. Ibid.

5. Pew Research Center Social & Demographic Trends, "Millennials: Unmoored from Institutions."

6. Pew Research Center, U.S. Politics & Policy, *Political Polarization in the American Public: How Increasing Ideological Uniformity and Partisan Antipathy Affect Politics, Compromise and Everyday Life*, June 12, 2014, http://www.people-press.org/2014/06/12/political-polarization-in-the-american-public/.

7. Edwards, *The Parties Versus the People*, 159.

8. David Schimke, "America's Transpartisan Future," interview with Michael Ostrolenk, *Utne Reader*, September–October 2009, http://www.utne.com/politics/americas-transpartisan-future-partisan.aspx.

Chapter 6. Mapping the Future

1. Cited in Edward Luce, *Time to Start Thinking: America in the Age of Descent* (New York: Grove Press, 2012).

2. Quoted in Drew Westen, *The Political Brain: The Role of Emotion in Deciding the Fate of the Nation* (New York: PublicAffairs, 2007), 156.

3. Ibid., 156.

4. George W. Bush, interview by Daryn Kagan, CNN, April 29, 2000.

5. Speech on election eve, 2008, in Chicago, Illinois.

6. Amy Mitchell et al., *Political Polarization & Media Habits*, Pew Research Center, Journalism & Media, October 21, 2014, accessed August 6, 2015, http://www.journalism.org/2014/10/21/political-polarization-media-habits/.

7. Cited in Jonathan Haidt, *The Righteous Mind: Why Good People Are Divided by Politics and Religion* (New York: Vintage Books, 2013), 305.

8. Conrad, *What You Should Know About Politics . . . but Don't.*

9. To hear Betsy McKinney's full transpartisan presentation, go to "Transpartisan Practices: Betsy McKinney," YouTube video, posted by Mediators Foundation, June 6, 2014, https://www.youtube.com/watch?v=NIGHOoaCTLM.

10. From personal interviews and correspondence with the author.

11. Donna Brazile, "A Place at the Table," *Ms. Magazine*, Winter/Spring 2014.

12. From a speech at the University of Massachusetts Boston, June 20, 2015. For a full view of Rajendra Sisodia's beyond-left-and-right economic perspective, go to http://www.mediatorsfoundation.org.

13. A. Lawrence Chickering and James S. Turner, *Voice of the People: The Transpartisan Imperative in American Life* (Goleta, CA: DaVinci Press, 2008).

14. From private correspondence with the author.

15. Andrew Ross Sorkin, "Hillary Clinton's Comment on Jobs Raises Eyebrows on Wall St.," *New York Times*, October 27, 2014.

16. Chris Cillizza, "Why Mitt Romney's '47 percent' comment was so bad," *Washington Post*, March 4, 2013, accessed November 6, 2015, http://www.washingtonpost.com/news/the-fix/wp/2013/03/04/why-mitt-romneys-47-percent-comment-was-so-bad/.

17. David Domke and Kevin Coe, *The God Strategy: How Religion Became a Political Weapon in America* (New York: Oxford University Press, 2007).

18. "Divine Rhetoric: God in the Inaugural Address," narrated by Scott Neuman, NPR, *It's All Politics*, January 22, 2013, accessed September 15, 2014, http://www.npr.org/sections/itsallpolitics/2013/01/22/169998659/divine-rhetoric-god-in-the-inaugural-address.

19. Cathy Lynn Grossman, "Poll: More Americans Want More Religion in Public Life," *OnFaith*, September 22, 2014, http://www.faithstreet.com/onfaith/2014/09/22/poll-more-americans-want-more-religion-in-public-life/34172.

20. Domke and Coe, *The God Strategy*, 11.

21. Remarks by Alan Abramowitz, "Conclave on Polarization," Big Sur, California, October 6, 2014, quoted in Steve McIntosh, "Reflections on Esalen's 2014 Conclave on Political Polarization," *Institute for Cultural Revolution Blog*, October 14, 2014, accessed July 22, 2015, http://www.culturalevolution.org/blog/reflections-on-esalens-2014-conclave-on-political-polarization/#.VbBYCqRVhBc.

22. Remarks by Michael Cromartie, "Conclave on Polarization," Big Sur, California, October 6, 2014, quoted in McIntosh, "Reflections on Esalen's 2014 Conclave on Political Polarization."

Conclusion

1. To meet this college freshman, go to https://www.youtube.com/watch?v=0a96fqZb_bA.

2. David Brooks, "Why Partyism Is Wrong," *New York Times*, October 28, 2014, http://www.nytimes.com/2014/10/28/opinion/david-brooks-why-partyism-is-wrong.html?_r=0.

3. I first shared this idea ten years ago in *Leading Through Conflict: How Successful Leaders Transform Differences into Opportunities* (Boston: Harvard Business Review Press, 2006), 231.

4. "The Universality of the Golden Rule in the World Religions," Teaching Values, accessed on July 29, 2015, http://www.teach ingvalues.com/goldenrule.html.

5. Martin Luther King Jr., "Where Do We Go from Here?" speech at Southern Christian Leadership Conference, Atlanta, Georgia, August 16, 1967, Famous Speeches and Speech Topics, http://www.famous-speeches-and-speech-topics.info/martin -luther-king-speeches/martin-luther-king-speech-where-do-we -go-from-here.htm.

6. Brooks, "The Thrill of Political Hating."

ACKNOWLEDGMENTS

Let me first acknowledge the scores of leaders, mentors, and pathfinders I cite in these pages. You are the flesh-and-blood reality of this emerging movement to reunite America. It is my honor and privilege to call you my colleagues and to be able to report on your work. Please consider your presence in this book as a form of acknowledgment of your work, which has given me hope, and of your inspiring leadership. Thank you for sharing your voice, experience, and wisdom in these pages.

I also want to express my appreciation to my colleagues who have introduced me to so many of the people and organizations profiled in these pages: Joan Blades, Allan Katz, Debilyn Molineaux, David Nevins, Amanda Roman, Michael Ostrolenk, and many other key allies. In particular, I am grateful for the passion of my friend, colleague, and partner in this work, John Steiner, which has inspired me for decades. With his remarkable wife and working ally, Margo King, John has supported the broader movement at every level. He has expanded both my understanding of it and my contact with it. Whenever my faith in the underlying unity of our country, and of life itself, wavered, our friendship helped restore it. I doubt this book would exist without him.

Beyond this inner circle, literally hundreds of friends and colleagues either participated in the title survey for this book or gave their feedback about both its contents and its language. It is absolutely a better book because of their engagement with it. I am particularly grateful to Robin Brody, Lawrence Chickering, Shane Gerzon, Tom Hast, Jordan Luftig, Betsy Hall McKinney, Eben Pagan, and Jim Turner for their comments that directly influenced the shape and content of this book. I also want to express specific thanks to Representative Mickey Edwards (R-Oklahoma), Representative David Skaggs (D-Colorado), Betty Sue Flowers, Peter Goldmark, Robert Strock, Juanita Brown, and David Isaacs, whose critiques of earlier versions of the book inspired me to dig deeper into myself and into the subject.

In addition, colleagues across the country—from Kansas City to Louisville, from Boston to the Bay Area—have hosted cross-partisan events that opened my eyes and touched my heart. Thank you for making your communities part of the journey of this book.

For over a quarter century, my base of operations has been Mediators Foundation. I extend my gratitude to every one of our board members, both those in body and those now in spirit, who over the years have supported our domestic and international bridge-building work. I want to personally acknowledge my colleague Rebecca Mendoza Nunziato, whose research significantly strengthened this book. You brought not only new insight but also a valuable millennial-generation perspective that immeasurably enriched my own.

Clearly, the team at Berrett-Koehler Publishers who birthed this book deserves a bow. After hearing several of my colleagues speak at a "Transpartisan Leadership" event that I moderated, publisher Steve Piersanti invited me to write this book. I hope you are pleased, Steve, with the result. While I am grateful for your inspiration as an editor, the responsibility is, as always, the author's.

Finally, I want to thank my wife, Melissa Michaels, who tended to our world with such care and love during the many months in which this book demanded my attention. Over the years of our marriage, you have helped me learn how to express myself more fully from my heart with you, which I believe helped me to do so on these pages as well. My gratitude extends to our children, our grandchildren, and our ever-expanding family, which ranges from Florida to California and Boston to Denver. Our diverse clan contains many of America's contradictions and contributions, wounds and wonders. The more we unite in love and support each other, the more I believe in the possibility of peace and unity for our country—and the world.

INDEX

abortion issue, 53–55
Affordable Care Act ("Obama-
 care"), 44, 60, 73, 98
Afghanistan, 3, 130
African Americans, 28
Ahmad, Aakif, 70, 85–86
Allsides.com, 31
American Bar Association's Divi-
 sion of Public Education,
 28
American Civil Liberties Union
 (ACLU), 66
American Conservative Union,
 75
American Enterprise Institute,
 101
American inventiveness and
 ingenuity, 157
American Public Square, 63
Americans for Tax Reform, 66,
 81, 140
AmericaSpeaks, 110
Anti-Defamation League, 45
Arendt, Hannah, 123
Arizona, 115–16
Arizona Republic, 115
Aspen Institute, 12, 121
authenticity, 61
Avlon, Jon, 96, 117

Bash, Dana, 25
Beck, Don, 132
Better World Society, 53
*Beyond Left and Right: Break-
 ing the Political Stalemate*
 (Chickering), 150
Bible, 67, 126, 148
Biden, Joe, 97
Bill of Rights, 113–14
Bipartisan Congressional
 Retreats, 12–13, 47, 71, 132
co-leaders, 58

ground rules, 56–59
Bipartisan Policy Center, 122, 154
Bipartisan Retreat Committee,
 12–13, 132
bipartisanship, 10, 25, 171n2
Blades, Joan, 42, 59–60, 62, 81
blame-the-other-party story line,
 49–50
body, metaphor of, 146–47
Boehner, John, 130
book titles, 10
bottom-up civic leadership, 35
boundary crossing, 118–19, 121
 connect with others, 166–67
boxing rhetoric, 48–49
Breakthrough Institute, 74
Bridge Alliance, 122, 134, 162,
 164
bridgeND, 1–2
bridging the partisan divide,
 157–58
 connect with others, 166–67
 fairness and freedom, 164–65
 getting involved, 160–61
 Golden Rules, 166–67
 identify leadership who
  reunite America,
  162–63
 joining or starting initiatives,
  163–64
 liberty to learn, 159–60
 love and power, 168–69
 transpartisan vacation,
  157–58
 vote for bridge-building candidates, 165–66
*Bringing Citizen Voices to the
 Table* (Lukensmeyer), 109
broken government, 104–7
Brooks, David, 160
Buckley, William, 150

Building Trust through Civil Discourse workshop, 112
Burstein, David, 96, 118
Bush, George H. W., 153
Bush, George P., 73
Bush, George W., 13, 92, 101-2, 111, 130, 132, 138
religion and, 153
Bush, George W. administration, 97-98
Bush, Jeb, 27, 73, 103, 151
businesspeople, 82-83

"Call to Prayer," 167
campaign finance, 104-5
Campaign for the Civic Mission of the Schools, 27-29
campaign-for-the-whole approach, 118-19
campaigning
as danger, 96, 97-107
endless, 15, 16, 102-4, 120
inspiring, 109, 117-20
campus-based activities, 1-2, 23, 36
candidates, effect of negative campaigning on, 46-48
capitals of states, 100
Cardenas, Al, 75
Carson, Rachel, 128
Celeste, Ted, 96, 111-12
center-right coalition, 107
Centrist Project, 115
centrists, 115
change, 147-48
Chasin, Laura, 42, 53-54, 161
Chickering, A. Lawrence, 133, 145, 150
Christian Coalition, 140
Christie, Chris, 106
citizen engagement, 108, 109-11
Citizen University, 34-36, 164
Citizens Campaign (New Jersey), 108
Civic Collaboratory, 34-36
civic disengagement, 99-100

civic engagement movement, 131
civic software, 138, 139-45
civil society, 9
civility, 6, 8, 12, 15, 36, 57
civility movement, 131
Cizik, Richard, 42, 66
Clayton, Eva, 12
Clean Air Act of 1970, 72-73
climate change, 72-74
Climate Change and Energy Security retreat, 22, 36-39
climate McCarthyism, 74
Clinton, Bill, 35, 48-49, 111, 138, 153
Clinton, Hillary, 103, 115, 151
Clinton-Bush-Obama administrations, 8
Coalition for Evidence-Based Policy, 87
Coalition for Public Safety, 81
Coburn, Tom, 89
Coelho, Tony, 102
Cole, Tom, 96, 116
co-leaders, 58
collaboration, 7, 11, 163
as opportunity, 80-93
Collins, Susan, 143
Colombe Foundation, 89-90
Commission on Presidential Debates (CPD), 105-6
commitment, 15
Common Cause, 140
Common Enterprise, 11
common ground, x, 1-2, 4, 7, 13-14, 17, 31, 61, 132
communication, shallow and ineffective, 45-46
Competitive Enterprise Institute (CEI), 37
compromise, 10
confirmation bias, 24-25
confirming, 15
danger of, 22, 23-27
Congress on your Corner event, 111

190   THE REUNITED STATES OF AMERICA

connection, as opportunity, 42,
    52–67
controlling, 15
    as danger, 42–52
Convergence Center for Policy
    Resolution, 85–86
Cooper, Jim, 101
Cornyn, John, 51
Cromartie, Michael, 154
Cronkite, Walter, 105
"cross spectrum" engagement,
    58–59
Culver, John, 105–6
curiosity, 61
#Cut50, 80–81
cybersecurity, 33–34, 43, 150
cynicism, 5–6, 26, 110

Daily Beast, 117
dangers, 19–20
    campaigning, 96, 97–107
    confirming, 22, 23–27
    controlling, 42–52
    position taking, 70, 71–80
Daschle, Tom, 111
Davis, Jake, 3–4, 50
debate, 90–91
    importance to democracy, 72
    presidential, 105–6
debate-dialogue chart, 91
decision makers, link to, 109
Defending America, Defend-
    ing Taxpayers retreat, 70,
    87–89
defense budget, 87–90
DeFoor, Allison, 73
Delaney, John K., 96, 116
deliberation, 17, 59, 110
democracy, 14–15, 17, 43–44,
    71–72, 93, 108–9
    laboratories of, 100, 112
democracy reform movement,
    131
Democratic Congressional Cam-
    paign Committee, 105
Democratic Party, 19, 74, 79

philosophy, 140–41
Department of Defense, 88
Desloge, Bryan, 42, 63
dialogue, 59, 91
dividing America, 99–107
divorce mediation, 60
Dole, Bob, 48–49, 140–41
domestic peace initiative, 60
domination, 43–44
Drier, David, 13
Drucker, Peter, 138
dynamic citizen engagement,
    108

E pluribus unum, 14–18, 19
    Public Square, 144–45
economic meltdown, 2008, 50
economic opportunity, 49–50
education, civic, 24–25, 27–29,
    31
Edwards, Mickey, 96, 120, 131
Eisenhower, Dwight, 88–89
election cycle promises, 10–11
elections
    partisan officials, 101–2
    trustworthy, 109, 113–17
    vote for bridge-building can-
        didates, 165–66
Emerson, Jo Ann, 13
EndPartisanship.org, 115
Environmental Protection
    Agency, 73, 128
Ethics and Public Policy
    Center, 154
Everyday Democracy, 63–64
exit poll comments, 46
exposure to new sources of
    information, 29–30

facilitated deliberation, 110
fairness, 56, 164–65
Faith and Politics Institute, 65, 167
faith-based organizations, 65–66
Federal Election Commission
    (FEC), 98–99, 102, 104,
    113, 114

Federalist Papers, 34
feedback, fast, 110
Fersh, Rob, 70, 85-86
firmness, 15
Forbes, Steve, 105
Foreign Affairs, 10
foreign policy, partisan, 3-4
Founding Fathers, 14, 31, 72,
    124, 152, 164
Founding Mothers, 164
Fowler, Tillie, 12
Fox News, 44-45
free enterprise, 147, 150-52
freedom, 15, 24
    order and, 147, 149-50
French Revolution, 139
Friedman, Tom, 18
friends first, 2
Future 500, 82-83, 86

Gable, John, 22, 30-31
Gallup, George, Jr., 153
Gallup polls, 126-27
Gates, Robert, 88-89
Gephardt, Dick, 12
gerrymandered districts, 7
Getting to Yes (Ury), 146
Giffords, Gabrielle, 110-11
Gingrich, Newt, 12, 70, 80-81,
    105, 162
global economy, 50
goals, 92
going beyond debate, 2
Golden Rule, 65, 167-68
Gore, Al, 13, 36-38, 101-2
governance, 17, 18
    broken government, 104-7
    effective, 109, 120-23
Government Accountability
    Board (Wisconsin), 113
government shutdown, 2013, 44
ground rules, 53, 55
    Bipartisan Congressional
        Retreat, 56-59
    Living Room Conversations,
        60-61

Political Journey, 112
Grumet, Jason, 96, 122
*Guardian of Democracy: The Civic
    Mission of Schools* report,
    27-28
gun policy, 76

Hamilton, Lee, 27-28
Harris, Katherine, 101, 102
Heierbacher, Sandy, 42, 59
Hinojosa, Ruben, 13
Hoffman, Gene, 76
Holder, Eric, 81
honesty, 9
Horwitz, Joshua, 77
hostility, 9
Houghton, Amo, 12
A House Divided (Gerzon), 11
Hudak, John, 77
Huffington, Arianna, 105
Hurricane Katrina, 109, 130
hyperpartisanship, 3, 6, 8-10,
    23-27, 37
    control and, 44
    democracy and, 72-73, 79
    economic opportunity, 49-50
    endless campaigning and, 104
    military conflict, 50-51
    presidency and, 97-98
    problem solving and, 50-51,
        93

idea catalyst, 3
identity, political, 112, 158,
    159-60
immigration, 74-76
Inconvenient Truth (Gore), 37
independence movement, 115-
    16, 126-31
    names for, 131-34
    venturing beyond partisan-
        ship, 134-35
Independents, 19, 42, 49, 115-
    16, 119
    rise of, 126-28
IndependentVoting.org, 115-16

informal get-togethers, 62
informed participation, 110
inner conservative and liberal, 5
inner partisanship, 13
inner-city gangs, 58
integrity, 9
interdependence, 142
Internet, 30-31
Internet privacy, 33-39
Iran, 130
Iraq, 3
Isaacson, Walter, 96, 120-21
ISIS, 50-51
It's Even Worse Than You Think (Ornstein), 44
It's Time Network, 142

Jackson, Jessica, 81
Jacobson, Nancy, 70, 92
Jamieson, Kathleen Hall, 26
Jefferson, Thomas, 126
Johnson, Paul, 116
Jones, Van, 70, 80-81, 162
Joyner, Liz, 42, 62-63
judgment, suspending, 61

Kansas City, 63
Katz, Allan, 42, 63
Kennedy, John F., 9, 78, 128
Kerry, John, 13
Killian, Linda, 96
Koch brothers, 81
Kull, Steven, 70, 86, 87

laboratories of democracy, 100, 112
LaHood, Ray, 12
leadership programs, 3-4
Leading Through Conflict: How Successful Leaders Transform Differences into Opportunities (Gerzon), 14
League of Women Voters, 105
learning, 17, 18, 61
   bridging the partisan divide, 159-60

exposure to new sources of information, 29-30
   as opportunity, 22, 27-32
left-right drama, 2-3
left-right line, 139-40, 144-45
Legislative Assembly (France), 139
liberty and authority, 147, 149
Liberty Coalition, 29, 66
Limbaugh, Rush, 9, 92-93
Lincoln, Abraham, 55, 126
listening, 56
Liu, Eric, 22, 34-36
Living Room Conversations, 60-61, 64, 81
local conflicts, 11
Long, Sean, 1-2, 4
Lott, John, 76
love, 55, 168-69
"loving our country," 42
loyalty, 9, 15
Lukensmeyer, Carolyn, 96, 109-11
Luntz, Frank, 106
Luzzatto, Tamera, 52-53, 104

manipulation, 26-27
marriage, interparty, 44
McCain, John, 13, 92, 98, 102
McConnell, Mitch, 51, 97
McCoy, Martha, 42, 64
McDaniel, Mark, 100-101
McKinney, Betsy Hall, 142
McKinney-Browning, Mabel, 22, 28
McKinnon, Mark, 70, 92-93
mediation, 60
Merz, Dini, 70, 89-90
military personnel, 3, 50-51
Mill, John Stuart, 140
millenials, 2, 82, 117-18
Millennial Action Project, 2
Molineaux, Debilyn, 162
Mondale, Walter, 140
Monroe, James, 152
Montgomery County school district, 64

MoveOn.org, 59-60, 66, 81, 110, 140
MSNBC, 44-45
Murray, Patty, 143

National Association of Evangelicals, 66
National Coalition for Dialogue & Deliberation (NCDD), 59, 164
national debt and deficit, 110
National Government Accountability Board, 114
National Institute for Civil Discourse (NICD), 110-11
national security, 87-90, 150
National Security Agency, 34
National Strategic Agenda, 92
negative campaigning, effect on candidates, 46-48
negative partisanship, 10
Nevins, David, 96, 121
New Evangelical Partnership for the Common Good, 65-66
New York Times, 103
news media
30-Day Media Fast, 29-30
boxing rhetoric, 48-49
defamatory commentary, 44-45
election headlines, 43
hyperpartisan, 25-26
shallow and ineffective commentary, 45
smart choices, 30
Next Generation, 111-12
Nixon, Richard, 9, 73, 128
No Labels, 84, 92-93, 121
nonpartisans, 18, 171n2
nonvoters, 19, 127
Nordhaus, Ted, 74
Norquist, Grover, 70, 81
Not So Divided America, A, 86

Obama, Barack, 9, 13, 51, 63, 130, 139
on free enterprise, 151-52
religion and, 153
Obama administration, 97-98
O'Connor, Sandra Day, 27-28, 111
Olbermann, Keith, 44-45
O'Neill, Tip, 8
Open Our Democracy Act, 116
openness, 56, 61
opinion polls, 7-8, 9
opportunity, 19-20
collaboration, 80-93
connection, 42, 52-67
learning, 22, 27-32
public service, 96, 107-22
O'Reilly, Bill, 44-45
Ornstein, Norm, 44, 101, 120
Ostrolenk, Michael, 22, 29-30, 66, 132
outside-of-the-box thinkers, 118

Panera Bread, 84
Parsons, Richard, 70, 87
participant diversity, 109
The Parties Versus the People (Edwards), 131
partisan divide
See bridging the partisan divide
partisanship, positive aspects, 8
partyism, 161
passion, 15
Patriot Act, 66
patriotic perspective, 67
patriotism, 160, 171n2
Paul, Rand, 33-34, 43, 150
Penn State University, 121
Pentagon Budget Campaign, 89-90
Pizarro, Shari, 100
pluralism, 18
polarity, 146-48
change and stability, 147-48

polarity (continued)
   freedom and order, 147,
      149-50
   liberty and authority, 147, 149
   public service and free enter-
      prise, 147, 150-52
   secularism and sanctity, 147,
      152-54
police officers, 28
Policy Consensus Initiative, 36
political clubs, 1-2, 35-36
political crisis, 7-8
Political Journey process, 112
Political Map 2.0, 143-44
Political Polarization in the American Public: How Increasing
   Ideological Uniformity and
   Partisan Antipathy Affect
   Politics, Compromise and
   Everyday Life study, 130
Pondiscio, Robert, 24-25
position taking, 15, 70
   as danger, 71-80
postpartisans, 8, 171n2
Pratt, Erich, 77
presidency, 102-4, 138-39
primaries, open, 115-19
prison population, 80-82
privacy, 56
problem solving, 17, 18
process, 54-55
Public Conversations Project,
   53-54, 64
public deliberation, 17
public service, 10, 96, 107-22
   free enterprise and, 147,
      150-52
   as opportunity, 96, 107-22
Public Square, 144
purposefulness, 61

Ravel, Anne M., 104
Reagan, Ronald, 8, 138, 152-53
rebuilding capacity to work
   together, 7-11
recommendations for action, 110

red and blue districts, 86
Reid, Harry, 50-51
relationship, 17, 18, 52-67
religion, 147, 152-54
Republican Party, 19, 75, 79
   philosophy, 140-41
respect, 9, 13, 56, 61, 163
responsibility, 35, 61
reuniting America, 99, 108, 132,
   156
Rodel Fellowship program,
   120-21
Roman, Amanda Kathryn, 96,
   107-8
Romney, Mitt, 13, 151-52
Roosevelt Institute Campus Network, 22, 36
Rowe-Finkbeiner, Kristin, 77
Rubio, Marco, 103
rules, 98-99
   See also ground rules
Run for America, 2, 118

Salit, Jackie, 96, 115-16
Salvi, John, 54
Sanders, Bernie, 27
Sandy Hook Elementary School
   shootings, 76, 77-78
Sawyer, Tom, 13
school, 24
Schultz, Howard, 52
Schumer, Charles, 116-17
secretary of state, 101-2
secularism, 147, 152-54
September 11 attacks, 88, 109,
   129
sex education, 32-33
Shaich, Ron, 70, 84
shared priorities, 110
Sharp, Gene, 132-33
Shellenberger, Michael, 74
Shireman, Bill, 70, 83
Silent Spring (Carson), 128
Sisodia, Rajendra, 143
Skaggs, David, 12
Smith, Marvin, 70, 82-83

snowball effect, 62
Snowden, Edward, 34, 150
social capital, 55
solopreneurs, 59
spin, 26-27, 87, 166
sporting events, 98, 101
stability, 147-48
stalemate, 43-44
state legislatures
    collaborative, 108
    divided, 100-101
Steiner, John, 132-34
Stenholm, Charles, 133
Story #1, 131
Story #2, 131
Story #3, x-xi, 7, 31, 64, 108,
    123-24, 131, 144, 147, 164
sworn-again, 35
Sworn-Again America, 35

Tallahassee, Florida, 62-63
Tanner, Doug, 42, 65
Tea Party, 73, 110
technology, 30-31
Tenth Amendment, 113-14
Texas, 73
Third Way, 115
30-Day Media Fast, 29-30
tipping point, 7-8
Tokaji, Daniel, 102
Transpartisan Leadership 101
    seminars, 159
transpartisan vacation, 157-58
transpartisan views, 154-56
transpartisans, 1, 62, 82-83,
    108, 131-34
    unity, search for, 154-56
Transportation Security Agency,
    34
tribalism, 44
trust, 163
    elections and, 109, 113-17

truth, 71, 87
Truth in Government, 87
Tucson shooting, 2011, 110-11
Turner, James S., 133, 145, 146
turning points, 11-14

Udall, Mark, 43
United Methodist Church, 65
United States Elections Project,
    100
unity, 14-15, 16
University Network for Collabor-
    ative Governance (UNCG),
    22, 36
University of California, Berke-
    ley, 150
Ury, William, 37, 146
US House of Representatives
    Bipartisan Congressional
        Retreat, 11-13, 47
    rising incivility project, 36
USA Patriot Act, 33

Village Square, 62-63, 64
Voice of the People, 86-87
Voice of the People: The Transpar-
    tisan Imperative in Ameri-
    can Life (Chickering and
    Turner), 133, 146

Wayne, John (the Duke), 9
What You Should Know About
    Politics . . . but Don't
    (political primer), 140-41
Wisconsin Legislature, 113
women's initiatives, 142-43
words, as weapons, 58

Yankelovich, Daniel, 9
yes-no, pro-con position taking,
    71-72
Young Invincibles, 2

ABOUT
THE AUTHOR

For a quarter of a century, Mark Gerzon has been a mediator, leadership consultant, and activist across the political divides. From Capitol Hill to capitals around the world, from divided communities to conflict-resolution workshops, he has been one of the architects of the movement to reunite America.

During the 1990s, Mark worked in divided communities to bring opposing factions into dialogue. The goal of the Common Enterprise, as the project, funded by the Rockefeller Foundation, was called, was to help communities develop a shared project that all competing groups agreed would serve the best interests of their *whole* community. Drawing from his grassroots experience across the country, he wrote *A House Divided: Six Belief Systems Struggling for America's Soul* (1996), which called for a "new patriotism" based on building bridges across the political spectrum rather than erecting walls.

Inspired by the message of that book, ten members of the US House of Representatives invited him, in collaboration with the Aspen Institute, to help design and facilitate the Bipartisan Congressional Retreats. Ever since those historic retreats in 1997 and 1999, he has been involved in many cross-party initiatives and off-site training workshops bringing together politicians from every party. He has also worked with scores of organizations active in cross-partisan work, ranging from the Federal Executive Institute to the Stennis Institute of Government to the Council for Excellence in Government.

Recognized for his expertise in fostering cross-party understanding, he was assigned by the United Nations Development Program to work with countries encountering election violence and partisan stalemate. Working with high-level party officials, he helped build the capacity for collaborative governance in Kenya, Nepal, and other emerging democracies.

After a decade of domestic and international trainings, he wanted to share what he had learned about the best practices for dealing with divisive issues and partisan politics. In 2006, in collaboration with Harvard Business Review Press, he published *Leading Through Conflict: How Successful Leaders Transform Differences into Opportunities*. His comprehensive overview defines the skills that can spark breakthrough innovation among even the most contentious, polarized stakeholders both in the United States and (through several translated editions) in countries around the world.

Despite progress in many segments of society, however, hyperpolarization in American politics worsened. Determined to highlight the heroic work of scores of organizations that were already tackling almost every aspect of this dangerous problem, Mark joined with a wide range of colleagues—Democrats, Republicans, Independents, and libertarians—to launch the Bridge Alliance (www.bridgealliance.us). This network of diverse, powerful organizations is working together to create a "third narrative" in American political culture: Americans working together.

For the last thirty years, Mark has also served as president of Mediators Foundation, a nonprofit organization dedicated to incubating projects that promote mutual understanding and the common good. The Foundation served as an institutional incubator for a wide variety of pioneering projects in the transpartisan field, including the Bridge Alliance, and also helped convene many of the issue dialogues described in this book. For more information about the Foundation or to support its work, please go to www.mediatorsfoundation.org.

Mark lives with his wife, the educator and author Melissa Michaels, in the foothills of the Rocky Mountains. He is the father of three sons and of two daughters by marriage, and is the grandfather of seven.

Berrett–Koehler
BK Publishers

Berrett-Koehler is an independent publisher dedicated to an ambitious mission: *Creating a World That Works for All*.

We believe that to truly create a better world, action is needed at all levels—individual, organizational, and societal. At the individual level, our publications help people align their lives with their values and with their aspirations for a better world. At the organizational level, our publications promote progressive leadership and management practices, socially responsible approaches to business, and humane and effective organizations. At the societal level, our publications advance social and economic justice, shared prosperity, sustainability, and new solutions to national and global issues.

A major theme of our publications is "Opening Up New Space." Berrett-Koehler titles challenge conventional thinking, introduce new ideas, and foster positive change. Their common quest is changing the underlying beliefs, mindsets, institutions, and structures that keep generating the same cycles of problems, no matter who our leaders are or what improvement programs we adopt.

We strive to practice what we preach—to operate our publishing company in line with the ideas in our books. At the core of our approach is stewardship, which we define as a deep sense of responsibility to administer the company for the benefit of all of our "stakeholder" groups: authors, customers, employees, investors, service providers, and the communities and environment around us.

We are grateful to the thousands of readers, authors, and other friends of the company who consider themselves to be part of the "BK Community." We hope that you, too, will join us in our mission.

A BK Currents Book

This book is part of our BK Currents series. BK Currents books advance social and economic justice by exploring the critical intersections between business and society. Offering a unique combination of thoughtful analysis and progressive alternatives, BK Currents books promote positive change at the national and global levels. To find out more, visit **www.bkconnection.com**.

Berrett–Koehler
BK Publishers
A community dedicated to creating
a world that works for all

Dear Reader,

Thank you for picking up this book and joining our worldwide community of Berrett-Koehler readers. We share ideas that bring positive change into people's lives, organizations, and society.

To welcome you, we'd like to offer you a free e-book. You can pick from among twelve of our bestselling books by entering the promotional code **BKP92E** here: http://www.bkconnection.com/welcome.

When you claim your free e-book, we'll also send you a copy of our e-newsletter, the *BK Communiqué*. Although you're free to unsubscribe, there are many benefits to sticking around. In every issue of our newsletter you'll find

- A free e-book
- Tips from famous authors
- Discounts on spotlight titles
- Hilarious insider publishing news
- A chance to win a prize for answering a riddle

Best of all, our readers tell us, "Your newsletter is the only one I actually read." So claim your gift today, and please stay in touch!

Sincerely,

Charlotte Ashlock
Steward of the BK Website

Questions? Comments? Contact me at bkcommunity@bkpub.com.

MIX
From responsible
sources
FSC® C113845

Certified

Corporation
bcorporation.net